Discovering

Pennsylvania

Discovering

Pennsylvania

Text: Lewis M. Paul
Concept and Design: Robert D. Shangle

First Printing February, 2001
American Products Publishing Company
Division of American Products Corporation
6750 SW 111th Avenue, Beaverton, Oregon 97008

"Learn about America in a beautiful way."

Library of Congress Cataloging-in-Publication Data

Paul, Lewis M., 1944
    Discovering Pennsylvania / text, Lewis M. Paul
      p. cm.
      ISBN 1-884958-68-0 (hardcover) – ISBN 1-884958-67-2 (pbk)
      1. Pennsylvania—Pictorial works. 2. Pennsylvania—Description and travel. 3.
    Pennsylvania—   History. I. Title

      F150 .P342001
      974.8—dc21   00-067518

Printed in Hong Kong by Palace Press
Concept, Publishing and Distribution by
American Products Publishing Company
Beaverton, Oregon USA

Contents

Introduction

Long before the land in this country became the priceless commodity it is today, people were fighting over it. The soft, green valleys of Pennsylvania were prized for their beauty and fertility by several contesting groups of settlers before, during, and after the Revolution. The Indians were mixed up in the land fuss, too, but in their battles with encroaching settlers, they were just doing what Indians all over the country were to do as the westward migration forced them off their territories. As early as 1682, settlers were moving into Pennsylvania, protected by the charter granted to William Penn by England's King Charles II as a payment for a monetary debt owed to Penn's father, Sir William Penn. Their occupancy in the Susquehanna Valley was challenged by groups of Connecticut Yankees seeking to annex the area to Connecticut. The French and Indian War was fought over portions of this territory, and later in time, some of the primary battles of the American Revolution took place here. Gettysburg has earned its place as one of the bloodiest of Civil War battlefields.

The Susquehanna Valley has seen its share of these land wars. The Susquehanna River, draining half the area of the state, is a stream often found within fabled lore important to both Native American and western cultures. Indian tribes of the Iroquois nation such as the Susquehannocks had long dwelt on its banks, raising crops in its fertile loam and feasting on the game of its enfolding forests. The valley has been one of the country's most exquisite examples of lush-river environment.

Such a gorgeous extent of river land stretching through the center of a now densely populated state should have largely disappeared beneath the factories and mills that line its shores after two centuries of settlement. But this has not happened. There are, of course, cities and industries situated along its shallow, rushing waters. However, for many of its sinuous miles, it consorts only with mountains and meadows, whose most numerous inhabitants are the richly diversified wildlife of the idyllic Susquehanna Valley.

The beauty of Pennsylvania's great river is just one aspect of the Keystone State's galaxy of enchantments. The state's good looks are partly a function of the Blue and Allegheny mountains that sweep diagonally across it, in ridge after ridge, from the southwest to the northeast, interrupted in any major way only by the lower Susquehanna River and its North and West branches. The low Alleghenies, rounded off by erosion and glacial pressures over uncounted eons, are a part of the long Appalachian chain that rules almost the whole eastern seaboard in from the coast and the Piedmont.

On the other hand, much of Pennsylvania's magic is man made. Not for just anything is it called the Keystone State. It was in the right place at the right time to play a crucial role in the nation's beginnings. And after we got started, the resources of the state and the vitality of its business enterprises were what kept us going. All around the state, there are places that keep reminding us of that. Hallowed parts of its old towns and cities have been carefully preserved or restored, glowing with their own kind of beauty as they become overlaid with the patina of age. Philadelphia, before all else, is history personified. It has managed to keep its traditions—and the nation's traditions—alive through a loving attention to the artifacts and symbols of the early struggles for independence that took place here. But the Quaker City is merely the most noteworthy example of the history that is behind almost every tree in Pennsylvania. Some of our most soul-wrenching dramas as a nation have been enacted upon its rolling countryside. First, our most famous battlefield, and second, the winter encampment of the Continental Army—Gettysburg and Valley Forge—are still there to remind a sometimes-jaded citizenry of what some of our forebears paid for dedication to a cause.

Most of Pennsylvania's border is a product of the Surveyor's art, being perfectly regular on the north, south, and west. In the northwest a narrow chimney of land borders Lake Erie. The Delaware River otherwise saves the state from being a perfect rectangle, which cuts down from the Catskill Mountains of southern New York and through the Kittantinny Mountains of Pennsylvania and New Jersey to form the grandly erratic eastern border. In a very general way, as to topography the Commonwealth of Pennsylvania may be divided into three regions. The southeast includes the plains and Piedmont country of the Delaware Valley, west as far as the Blue Mountains. From the south-central border up toward the northeast, the Allegheny Mountains form a wide highland. The western third is high, rolling plateau country, with an exception for the plains of the Lake Erie shore.

The Pennsylvania scene is most varied. It encompasses every conceivable kind of terrain except the extremes such as the highest, lowest, wettest, driest, and so forth found in the state. Its natural resources are staggering. Some states in the Union that are far larger in area are poverty stricken by comparison. West of the Alleghenies and below ground level are immense deposits of bituminous coal, high quality coking coal. Pennsylvania-grade oil comes from the west too, a high quality lubricating oil of unsurpassed excellence. In the east the coal mines around Scranton and Reading and Pottsville yield up the hard black rocks called anthracite. Clean burning anthracite coal is found nowhere else in the world. But underground Pennsylvania is far from the whole story. The surface is no small potatoes either, to use an agricultural image. The overlays of limestone soil in some parts of the state make farming an extremely worthwhile enterprise. Lancaster County, in the Pennsylvania Dutch country of the southeast, has out produced any other area of equal size ever since the "Dutch" began farming the land.

Dense forests, both hardwoods and conifers cover half of Pennsylvania. The great range of plant life includes species that normally grow in other regions, as in the southern states and in the Mississippi Valley. The diversity of wildlife puts it in the front rank of states in this regard. Some of its larger animals, such as moose and elk, disappeared in the days when logging and animal slaughter were unregulated. Over the past many years, the state has carried out extensive reforestation and reintroduced some vanished species. So the fishy, furry, and feathery kinds of animals are now deployed in strength throughout a vast and vigorous forest kingdom.

The extent of natural beauty in Pennsylvania is sometimes surprising to outsiders and visitors to the state. Even persons who were born in Pennsylvania continue to be astonished by its visual enchantments. Such a situation seems to be helped along as many Pennsylvanians tend to cluster within a handful of big cities like Philadelphia, Pittsburgh, Erie, Harrisburg, Scranton, Allentown, and Altoona. That leaves the balance of the population spread over a large area. Pennsylvania has many small towns, some as old as the state itself, retaining the riches of smallness during all that time.

Pennsylvania, then, could be labeled as a somewhat paradoxical

Commonwealth. It has historically been a place of refuge for anyone seeking tolerance for a way of life and willing to allow others the same right. It is an old land and a new land tied together. It is a jumble of factories and mines, and crowded cities; and it is a quiet wilderness of lovely rivers, soft blue-green mountains, and pine-scented forests. It is truly a combination of many things, and in its contradictions and harmonies, perhaps in Pennsylvania may be found the answer to the Great Spirit of the United States.

Important Facts

Preamble to the Constitution

*We, the people of the Commonwealth of Pennsylvania,
grateful to Almighty God
for the blessings of civil and religious liberty,
and humbly invoking His guidance,
do ordain and establish this Constitution.*

Entered the Union:
December 12, 1787,
Second State
Capital: Harrisburg

State Animal: Whitetail Deer

State Bird: Ruffed Grouse

State Dog: Great Dane

State Fish: Brook Trout

State Flagship: *U. S. Brig Niagara*

State Flower: Mountain Laurel

State Tree: Eastern Hemlock

The Dynamic West

The western side of Pennsylvania has had, as the east side has had, a crucial role in the state's development. Geographically, historically, and economically, it has long been a keystone area of the *Keystone State*. In the 19th century, Pennsylvania was *the* business leader of the nation. That preeminence came about, in part, because of the mineral and fossil fuel wealth that underlay its surface, particularly west of the Appalachian Mountains. Colonel Edwin L. Drake discovered oil at Titusville in northwest Pennsylvania on August 28, 1859. Oil became evident at a depth of 69.5 feet, giving rise to one of the biggest industries in Pennsylvania. Soon oil wells appeared all over the upper western region, and the flow from the wells was enough for Pennsylvania to have produced sixty percent of the nation's oil through the turn of the century. One well in particular has achieved an historic standing that requires special attention, the McClintock Well #1, the oldest producing oil well in the world. It was originally drilled in August, 1861, and it still produces oil today. The Bowers brothers, John and Joe, operated the well through the late 1890s, followed by a son who sold in 1919. According to *The Oil Country Gazette* (Vol. 11, No. 1 by Susan J. Beates) Quaker State Oil Corporation ultimately became the owner of the famous well, and in 1998 the well was donated "to the Colonel, Inc., Drake Well Museum's Associates Group." The McClintock Well #1 is now a part of the Pennsylvania Historical and Museum Commission, under the administration of the Drake Well Museum in Titusville. A real hands-on experience is available at the Drake Well Museum, the site where Edwin Drake drilled the world's first oil well. The constant sound of a true oil operation is ongoing at the museum. A replica of the original well is there and the museum states that "Outdoor exhibits of oilfield machinery in our 219-acre park setting along Oil Creek include a working central power lease with rodlines and pumping jacks, a 100 [year] old pumping station, and an early steel drilling rig." The area is ripe with historical information regarding the oil industry.

Oil Creek State Park houses many miles of area once covered with oil drilling rigs, most mines now capped, and some still alive but not operating. This area brims to the top with colorful history that calls to be investigated. A train trip is available within the park that travels through the many historic landmarks. Money was made, lots of money; and money was lost, lots of money. "Colorful" towns such as Pithole, Rouseville, Funkville, Petroleum City, Plumer, Titusville, and Oil City were created in a hurry, inhabited by many thousands of people in a short period of time following the big "discovery." And most of those towns all but vanished as fire and flood took their toll. As the oil glut dwindled, so did the people. Visitor centers and many museums in the area are rich with information regarding the oil fields of the region. Titusville on the north end and Oil City on the south end sandwich Oil Creek State Park, where oily slicks once rose to the surface of the water providing an iridescent hue. For several hundred years prior to the discovery of underground oil, Native Americans gathered oil along Oil Creek, using the material for medicinal and cosmetic needs. Multitudes of oil companies were developed by entrepreneurial minds, some growing to vastness and some silently vanishing. The oil fields long ago yielded supremacy to the giants of the Southwest, but Pennsylvania crude is still being pumped, its fine quality as a lubricating oil recognized in several well known industry trade names. Oil is still important to Pennsylvania's economy.

Long before oil was discovered in Pennsylvania, the enormous bituminous coal fields of the "Pittsylvania country" had been discovered and were being worked. The coal vein underlying western Pennsylvania is so enormous that nearly all of the nation's production comes from this area along with West Virginia and Kentucky. The iron ores of the region, now fairly well depleted, helped to launch Pittsburgh as the nation's "Steel City" in the 19th century. The area's steel mills now get their ore from out of state, some of them from Michigan's Upper Peninsula.

All this information should reinforce the point that western Pennsylvania represents wealth. Pittsburgh has several advantages for success. Its strategic geographic position astride the Allegheny and Monongahela rivers, and being located center stage where the two rivers converge creating the Ohio River, provides the foundation to a sound economic base. Pittsburgh's strategic position as a gateway to the interior of the country started the area off with flourish on its career as a center of industry. The competition of the railroad giants—the Pennsylvania and the Baltimore & Ohio—to breach the Appalachian Mountains, along with the activities of Andrew Carnegie, George Westinghouse, Andrew Mellon, and other financial and industrial wizards also helped establish the western region and the city of Pittsburgh as a powerful center of commerce.

But the drive and the spirit of the people have been reflected in other ways besides the sober ones of business and industry. Reminders of some of the colorful events of the past are still very much in evidence. Take Brownsville for example. It is an industrial town south of Pittsburgh on a hill by the Monongahela River. In the 19th century, it was busy forging iron. Before that, indeed, shortly after Brownsville became a town in 1785, a circle of communities in the area, with Brownsville taking the lead, launched the so-called Whiskey Rebellion in July 1791. One of the chief products of the western country at the time was whiskey. It was so plentiful that it was identified as a medium of monetary exchange. Farmers distilled the grain, and the finished product was many times more valuable by bulk than the original grain. First the state, then the federal government, levied a tax on the whiskey. Not only did this tax lower the profits from the sale of whiskey shipped across the mountains to the east, the government levied a higher tax on the locally held whiskey. Local leaders began to protest the excise tax as discriminatory. So the Whiskey Rebellion was on. Besides Brownsville, the settlements of Washington and Ginger Hill (now known as Slippery Rock) were among other towns that got into the act, refusing to pay the tax and roughing up the tax collectors. It was a very emotional issue since whiskey was, literally, the lifeblood of the people. The Whiskey Rebellion soon gave up, having been faced with opposition from Pittsburgh residents who may have been pressured to change the minds about the tax by eastern influence. The force that swayed the rebels was most likely a massive show by the federal government. In August, 1794, some 13,000 federal troops were sent to Uniontown to collect the tax, and otherwise, to get things under control. Ginger Hill, by the way, was named for the practice of the town's tavern keeper of adding Jamaica ginger to the whiskey that he dispensed. This was not for flavor but to enhance the color of watered-down whiskey.

Even with all of the coal and oil lodged in those hills, there is plenty of natural beauty to go around. In the north, directly in the middle of the oil and gas-well region, is the 1,000-square-mile Allegheny National Forest. Most of this forest is prime woodland. Towns are present, but they are small and unobtrusive. Hundreds of miles of winding roads penetrate the forest, connecting the towns and

Independence Hall, Philadelphia, Southeastern Pennsylvania

Independence Hall is easily identified with terms such as Freedom, Human Rights, Liberty, Pursuit of Happiness, and Equality. These words are imbedded in the ambiance of this fine old building, constructed between the years of 1732 and 1753. Designed to be the Pennsylvania State House, it became the center of America's struggle for righteous treatment; for the recognition to produce and maintain national interest within the boundaries of the American colonies, separate from England. History regarding a *new country* took mold within Independence Hall. Famous patriots struggled within the walls of this building, believed by many to be the most important building in American history.

Photography by James Blank

17

Gettysburg National Military Park, Gettysburg, South-central Pennsylvania

This is the site of a most incredible battle fought between citizens of the United States of America, The Battle of Gettysburg; a Civil War battle, often referred to as a war between the states, or a war between the North and the South. It is difficult to determine who was the victor at Gettysburg. The battle commenced on July 1, 1863, and was bitterly fought for three days. Records indicate that 3,155 Union soldiers were killed over those three days, while Confederate numbers have an estimate of 2,600 to 4,500 soldiers killed. Of those killed, wounded and missing soldiers over the duration of the battle, the Union forces number about 23,000 and the Confederate numbers generate from some 20,000 to 25,000 soldiers. Though the battle was considered a turning point for the pending victory by the Union forces in the Civil War, which concluded two years later, the damage and destruction to the soldiers and to the local people was immense. The serene beauty found in the area, today, makes all the more poignant its role in our nation's struggle for equality. Some 1,400 monuments are located on the 6,000 rolling acres of ground that create the National Battlefield. In the National Cemetery of the battlefield park, the Soldier's National Monument marks the site of some brief remarks by President Abraham Lincoln on November 19, 1863, known as the Gettysburg Address.

Photography by James Blank

The Betsy Ross House, 239 Arch Street, Philadelphia, Southeast Pennsylvania

Elizabeth (Betsy) Griscom and John Ross opened their upholstery shop in this rented house on Arch Street in 1775. The two-and-one-half story Georgian-style house was built around 1740. Betsy, whose husband was killed in 1776 while guarding ammunition, was secretly commissioned by the Continental Congress in May, 1776, to sew the first flag of the new nation, which she completed in June. The following year "on June 14, 1777, the Continental Congress, seeking to promote national pride and unity, adopted the national flag. 'Resolved: that the flag of the United States be thirteen stripes, alternate red and white; that the union be thirteen stars, white in a blue field, representing a new constellation.' "

Photography by James Blank

National Memorial Arch, Valley Forge National Historical Park, Valley Forge, Northwest of Philadelphia

As the National Park Service states, "In the late nineteenth century, the narrative of Valley Forge inspired private citizens to begin the effort to preserve the site of General [George] Washington's soldiers' camp as a memorial. Formal recognition for the troops who wintered at Valley Forge came when the Pennsylvania legislature designated the area as a state park in 1893. Valley Forge officially became part of the national park system in 1977. Today, the mission of the National Park Service at Valley Forge is to preserve, protect and maintain the natural and cultural resources that are associated with and commemorate the encampment of the Continental Army in 1777-1778 and educate the American people about one of the most defining events in the nation's history."

Photography by James Blank

Daniel Boone Homestead, Berks County, Southeast of Reading, Southeast Pennsylvania

Administered by the Pennsylvania Historical and Museum Commission, the Daniel Boone Homestead has been owned by the state of Pennsylvania since 1938. Of the 579 acres that comprise the current homestead, 250 acres were originally purchased by Daniel Boone's parents, Squire and Sarah Morgan Boone, in 1730. Squire constructed a single room, one-story log house over a cellar and spring. Daniel was born in 1734, joining five other siblings, and was the sixth of eleven children. The Boone family left their home in 1750 and moved to North Carolina. The land was purchased by William Maugridge in 1750 and sold to John DeTurk in 1770, following the death of Maugridge in 1766. Enlarged from the simple one-room and one-story appearance, the house has experienced sizeable expansion and renovation from the days of Daniel Boone. A portion of the handsome two-story stone building rests on the original log-house foundation and cellar, and it includes a *newer section* built in the mid- to late 1700s that is fronted by the long porch. The Pennsylvania Historical and Museum Commission states that the Homestead grounds includes "seven eighteenth-century structures, a lake, picnic areas and other recreational facilities. The site interprets . . . through exhibits, programs tours and publications." An abundant amount of wildlife frequents the area as well as many species of birds. Known as a frontiersman, Daniel maintained a prominent position in the Kentucky Territory, remembered for his daring deeds protecting the settlers from pressuring Indian skirmishes and exploring territory for westward expansion.
Photography by Robert D. Shangle

Hopewell Furnace National Historic Site, Elverson, south of Reading, Southeast Pennsylvania

As an example of 19th-century entrepreneur achievement, Hopewell Furnace represents the iron industry of early Pennsylvania. The National Park Service says that "Hopewell Furnace National Historic Site is one of the finest examples of a rural American 19th-century iron plantation. The buildings include a blast furnace, the ironmaster's mansion, and auxiliary structures. Hopewell Furnace was founded in 1771 by Ironmaster Mark Bird. The furnace operated until 1883." French Creek State Park surrounds the historic site, preserving "the lands the furnace utilized for its natural resources." More than iron forging occurred on the plantation. As a true Pennsylvania community, families lived on the Hopewell Furnace grounds. Men worked the iron, but there were many other jobs that were performed, necessary to support the plantation community. "The lives of the people, from the men who made the iron to the women who supplied the everyday necessities for living, can be examined [here]. These people include furnace workers, wood cutters, colliers [charcoal makers], miners, farmers, maids, and teamsters. This diverse work force supported Hopewell Furnace through 112 years of iron making history."
Photography by Shangle Photographics

The Adam Miller Farmstead, Somerset Historical Center, Somerset, Southwest Pennsylvania

Well defined history of Somerset County is found at Somerset Historical Center, a place where history is quickened and you can feel the true adventure of it, as if part of the current activity of the day. The grounds include original buildings that were constructed in the 1800s, relocated to provide a hands-on portrayal of the life style of their inhabitants. Adam Miller built his log house in rural Pennsylvania around 1800, along with a smokehouse and a log barn. Each is equipped with furnishings typical of the times. The 1859 Walter's Mill Bridge, listed on the National Register of Historic Places, adds a touch of completeness to the 19th-century scene, along with an authentic display of an 1850s Maple Sugar Camp that illustrates and explains the tools, equipment, and the methods of production necessary to create maple products. Somerset County, a leading producer in maple products, is rich in maple trees, and from late February through April, when freezing nights and warm days cause the sap to run in the maple tree, it is time to collect the sap and process the liquid. The replicated 1876 General Store takes you back to the old-fashioned post office, penny candy, and the atmosphere of early Pennsylvania. Exhibits of agricultural and industrial equipment are present, along with the Visitor Center that provides period-dated exhibits, guided tours, and an excellent gift shop for memento seekers. A Genealogical Library is also available.

Photography by Robert D. Shangle, Courtesy of the Somerset Historical Center

Presque Isle Lighthouse, Presque Isle State Park on Lake Erie at Erie, Northwest Pennsylvania

Pennsylvania can boast of having three lighthouses at Erie, one on Erie Bay known as the Erie Land Light (Old Presque Isle) built in 1867 and located in Dunn Park; the North Pier Light constructed in 1927 that guards the entrance of Presque Isle Bay; and the Presque Isle Light on Lake Erie within Presque Isle State Park. The need for the Presque Isle Light was established in 1872 and the construction was completed in July, 1873. The lightkeeper's residence was attached to the original forty-foot square brick tower, which has since been raised to the current sixty-eight feet. Still an active and operational light that was automated in 1962, the lighthouse is maintained by the Coast Guard, but the living quarters is now a private residence.

Photography by Robert D. Shangle

General George Washington's Headquarters, Valley Forge National Historical Park Valley Forge

Successful battles and campaigns are rarely won without extensive planning. It was from this house that General Washington and his staff conducted the daily routine of the army while wintering his troops. Often there were more than twenty officers and aides present to assist the Commander-in-Chief in his duties. They also spent much time strategizing methods for victory over the British in this house owned by Isacc Potts. Records indicate that when General Washington occupied the house, he paid his landlord one-hundred pounds Pennsylvania hard-coin currency as rent money for a period covering six months. His wife, Martha, joined him in Valley Forge in February, 1778, just before his forty-fifth birthday. General Washington occupied the house until June, 19, 1778, at which time he and the Continental Army marched on to Monmouth, New Jersey, engaging in a battle with the British on June 28th, known as the Battle of Monmouth. The house is open for tours and includes some original items owned or used by General Washington. Much of the furnishings are period pieces and provide an excellent opportunity to view life as it was in Washington's time of occupancy.

Photography by Robert D. Shangle

The pumpkin patch near Elverson, South of Reading, Southeast Pennsylvania

It is pumpkin time in Chester County, Pennsylvania, where fields and fields of pumpkins add a glow to the already shimmering colors of autumn. This area of Pennsylvania is often referred to as the Pennsylvania Dutch Country, where folks who cherish a more plain life style choose to live. That plain life style most often refers to the religious group known as the Amish, yet it does include the Mennonites and the Brethren. The Amish farms are often identified by the lack of "modern" conveniences such as self-powered equipment as in automobiles and tractors, and the electricity that most people can hardly live without. Beautifully groomed fields are prepared by draft animals and manual field implements; miles of those fields are spread across the rolling hills and lands of Pennsylvania. Big white houses and handsome farm buildings dot the landscape. To some, life may appear plain, but it is a rewarding life style to anyone who gazes upon the perfection achieved by the efforts of those who persevere to their commitments.
Photography by Shangle Photographics

McConnell's Mill State Park on Slippery Rock Creek, Lawrence County, West Pennsylvania

The mill was built in 1868 and purchased by Thomas McConnell in 1875, who upgraded its efficency by "replacing the waterwheel with water turbines and rolling mills," doing away with the grinding stones. The mill was operational until 1928. The creek flows through Slippery Rock Gorge, named for rocks that once were made slippery by seeping oil that coated their surface.

Photography by Shangle Photographics

Historic Christ Church, Philadelphia, Southeast Pennsylvania

Christ Church was built between 1727 and 1754, the religious home to such notables as George Washington, Betsy Ross, and Benjamin Franklin. The 1719 cemetery, located a short distance from the church, was first owned by William Penn who refused to sell it. Following Penn's death, his wife sold the property, stating: "Let the Anglicans have it. They can be buried in the woods." Today the cemetery is located in one of the more densely populated areas in the city, and the country. Franklin and his wife, as requested, were buried in the farthest corner away from the front of the cemetery; however, today the site is next to an iron fence that is bordered by a concrete sidewalk and two busy streets.

Photography by Shangle Photographics

Fort Necessity National Battlefield, East of Uniontown in Fayette County, Southwest Pennsylvania

It was July 3, 1754, when events drastically changed the life of young George Washington, then twenty-one years old. The National Park Service describes the event well: "The confrontation at Fort Necessity in the summer of 1754 was the opening battle of the war fought by England and France for control of the North American continent. It was also the opening episode of a worldwide struggle known in North America as the French and Indian War and elsewhere as the Seven Years' War. It ended in 1763 with the expulsion of French power from North America and India. The action at Fort Necessity was also the first major event in the military career of George Washington, and it marked the only time he ever surrendered to an enemy." As a young lieutenant colonel, Washington, loyal to the British, assumed command of a Virginia Regiment when the commanding officer, Joshua Fry, died. He was then promoted to colonel. Arriving at what was known as the Great Meadow, Washington and his men established an encampment. Days of killing skirmishes ensued between the French and the Virginian soldiers. Following the conflict Washington "built a circular palisaded fort, which he called Fort Necessity." Following the battle of July 3, the defeated British troops returned to Virginia and the French burned Fort Necessity.

Photography by Robert D. Shangle

The city of Pittsburgh, Southwest Pennsylvania

The "heart of a nation" are words that may best describe what Pittsburgh has been to America, what it is today, and what it will be tomorrow. Its strategic location, situated on three major rivers in the eastern section of the United States, provides a primary transportation route through lands that produce important commodities for the country and the world. It is speculated that the Native American was the first to frequent the land; then the French and British made an appearance, all three factions aware of the importance of the land known as the "Golden Triangle." The Allegheny River on the north and the Monongahela River on the south merge at the tip of the land forming the Ohio River. The French built two forts over time, remembered as Fort DuQuesne; the British also built two forts, the last between 1759 and 1761 after the French fled the area and burned their fort when they knew they were out numbered by an oncoming foe. Fort Pitt was built, named for Britain's Prime Minister William Pitt. Today Point State Park and Fort Pitt occupy the famous location. Grown from a small military fort to a mega-metropolis, Pittsburgh has struggled through the hard times, breaking through to the good times. Coal and steel were the backbone of economic success for Pittsburgh and the surrounding area. Manufacturing industries established themselves, producing such things as glass, rope, boats, and iron products. People with names long remembered appeared on the scene, providing jobs, inventing new products, and initiating medical breakthroughs: Andrew Carnegie, John Heinz, Andrew Mellon, John Roebling, Vladimir Zworykin, Jonas Salk, George Westinghouse; the list can go on and on. Founded in 1787 the University of Pittsburgh once held center stage but is now joined by ten other state accredited centers for higher learning.
Photography by Shangle Photographics

The Soldiers Memorial in the National Cemetery, Gettysburg National Military Park, Southeast Pennsylvania

It was at this site on November 19, 1863, that President Abraham Lincoln delivered his famous Gettysburg Address : *Fourscore and seven years ago our fathers brought forth on this continent a new nation, conceived in liberty and dedicated to the proposition that all men are created equal. Now we are engaged in a great civil war testing whether that nation, or any nation so conceived and so dedicated, can long endure. We are met on a great battlefield of that war. We have come to dedicate a portion of that field as a final resting-place for those who here gave their lives that that nation might live. It is altogether fitting and proper that we should do this. But, in a larger sense, we cannot dedicate — we cannot consecrate — we cannot hallow — this ground. The brave men, living and dead, who struggled here have consecrated it far above our poor power to add or detract. The world will little note, nor long remember what we say here, but it can never forget what they did here. It is for us the living, rather, to be dedicated here to the unfinished work which they who fought here have thus far so nobly advanced. It is rather for us to be here dedicated to the great task remaining before us — that from these honored dead we take increased devotion to that cause for which they gave the last full measure of devotion — that we here highly resolve that these dead shall not have died in vain — that this nation, under God, shall have a new birth of freedom — and that government of the people, by the people, for the people, shall not perish from the earth.*
Photography by James Blank

31

The City Hall Building in downtown Philadelphia

Across beautiful Love Park, officially titled the John F. Kennedy Park, is the handsome City Hall building that maintains a capital position among the modern structures of today's architectural giants. Built in 1901 to French Second Empire architectural specifications, the masonry structure is the tallest of its kind, with forty-two stories, topped by a 37-foot statue of William Penn, and it has" the most comprehensive sculptural decoration of any American building." Interior tours are available. An eclectic architectural montage could well describe the central downtown area of Philadelphia. The original charm of the historic, classic buildings meld with the sleek, progressive lines of new-image generation of architectural achievement.

Photography by Shangle Photographics

"On to their destination," an Amish husband and wife near the city of Lancaster, Southeast Pennsylvania

Drive your vehicle slowly and with a cautious attitude as you drive through Lancaster County, for this is Amish country. Yellow caution signs are posted on state and county roads that display a silhouette of a horse-drawn buggy, alerting the automobile driver to the probability of an Amish buggy. The rolling hills and well trimmed farms conspire to slow down a sight-seeing automobile driver who can then better enjoy the pastoral view and lessen a chance of an unpleasant meeting with a horse and buggy. As a religious group, the Amish live by an age-old code that has provided well for the people and still brings pride to their community. Though most "modern" conveniences are not part of their life style, they are willing to make change when it is prudent to do so, and as long as that change does not alter their simplistic way of living and interfere with family life. Simplicity in dress is mandated, as plain dark colors are chosen for clothing. Adult married men wear beards, no mustache is allowed, and a black hat or broad-brimmed straw hat; married women wear a white apron and white pray covering. Children attend school through the eighth grade.
Photography by James Blank

Old Stone House, Slippery Rock in Butler County, Western Pennsylvania

Here is a house with a colorful history. It was originally built by John K. Brown in 1822 as a resting place for weary travelers, often referred to in those days as a tavern. Food and lodging was available in the three-story building. The "colorful" portion of its history refers to the murdering Mohawk Indian who in 1843 drank too much liquor in the tavern and went out and killed a mother and her five children. He was hung in 1844. A group of men appeared in the 1840s who frequented the tavern, and they were creating counterfeit silver coins. Diptheria struck, killing the apparent leader, and the passing of counterfeit silver coins died too. Business began to fail and the building was abandoned. Deterioration set in and rubble was left. A restoration program was implemented in the 1960s that has given renewed life to the building, establishing it as an important historical landmark in the area. The Slippery Rock University History Department manages the museum and arranges for tours. The University began its career in 1889 as Slippery Rock Normal School, preparing young people for a life of teaching. Name changes always take place and there was no exception here: Slippery Rock State Teachers College and Slippery Rock State College were names preceding today's title: Slippery Rock University. The city of Butler, county seat of Butler County, can boast of being the town where the "jeep" was developed, the great automobile used by the army beginning in World War II. West of Butler is Portersville and the Portersville Steam Show that displays old fashioned steam-powered tractors. Lake Arthur is nearby offering a boaters paradise.

Photography by Shangle Photographics

Old Bedford Village, Bedford, South-central Pennsylvania

A visit to Old Bedford Village is like a step *back in time*. Rich in history regarding a typical 19th-century life style is represented through a living history atmosphere. The Village describes itself by stating, "Over 40 log and stone homes, schoolhouses, craft shops, and friendly settlers surround you with the reality of history. . . . Every building at Old Bedford Village has a past and personality just waiting to be discovered." The village smithy clangs his hammer, and activities of bustling house dwellers illustrate the daily needs of the village dwellers in this history center.
Photography by Robert D. Shangle

35

Oil Creek State Park, south of Titusville, Northwest Pennsylvania

The State Park describes itself best: "Located in Crawford and Venango counties, the 7,096 acres of park land consist of deep hollows, steep hills, wetlands and a beautiful, meandering creek through 13.5 miles of the scenic Oil Creek Gorge. Remains of the oil boom days still exist in the park hidden among clean trout waters, hemlock and broadleaf forest, and a wide variety of plant and animal life. . . . The primary purpose of [the park] is to tell the story of the changing landscape." The park is located between Drake Well Museum and Titusville on the north side and Oil City on the south side. Hiking trails are abundant, as well as a paved bicycle path that is often used for cross-country skiing during the snow months. Canoeing, fishing, and hunting are available for the taking. It is a fine place for a family picnic. Here is an excellent location to learn about Pennsylvania's petroleum industry. The Petroleum Oil Center is a museum that explains well the activities of one of Pennsylvania's rich and colorful histories. Photographs, literature, and museum guides are available for information.

Photography by Robert D. Shangle

Erie Maritime Museum and the *U. S. Brig Niagara*, **Erie, Northwest Pennsylvania**

The handsome Erie Maritime Museum is home port for the reconstructed *U. S. Brig Niagara*, the ship Commodore Oliver Hazard Perry boarded when his own vessel, the flagship *Lawrence*, was damaged during the Battle of Lake Erie on September 10, 1813. The hull of the *Niagara* was raised in 1913 from the watery depths of Misery Bay in Lake Erie where it had been scuttled in 1820. It was restored and displayed, honoring the ship at a centennial tribute of the Battle of Lake Erie. Beginning in 1987 a massive renovation took place to restore the vessel to the finest of conditions, declaring the ship to be the Official Flagship of the Commonwealth of Pennsylvania. The city of Erie has been declared the Flagship City as well. The ship is available for tours and sailing excursions. The Maritime Museum provides a hands-on experience of Erie's maritime history, which includes exhibits of reconstructed sections of Perry's first flagship, the *Lawrence*.

Photography by the courtesy of the Erie Maritime Museum

At Historic Hanna's Town, Westmoreland County, north of Greensburg, Southwest Pennsylvania

When Westmoreland County was formed on February 26, 1773, Robert Hanna was named judge over the first county seat west of the Allegheny Mountains. His complex became known as Hanna's town, today appearing as a reconstruction of a place where history was made, and hard cold decisions were made by determined citizens of the Massachusetts Colony. On May 16, 1775, people of the area gathered at Hanna's Town determined to come to a consensus regarding the violation of people's rights by the British. A written instrument was drafted and became known as *Hanna's Town Resolves*. A portion of the Resolves follows: " 'Resolved unanimously, That the Parliament of Great Britain, by several late acts, have declared the inhabitants of Massachusetts Bay to be in Rebellion, and the ministry, by endeavoring to enforce those acts, have attempted to reduce the said inhabitants to a more wretched state of slavery than ever before existed in any state or country. Not content with violating their constitutional and chartered privileges, they would strip them of the rights of humanity, exposing lives to the wanton and unpunishable sport of licentious soldiery, and depriving them of the very means of subsistence." . . . "Resolved unanimously, That there is no reason to doubt that the same system of tyranny and oppression will (should it meet with success in Massachusetts Bay) be extended to every other part of America: It is therefore become the indispensable duty of every American, of every man who has any public virtue or love for his country, or any bowels for posterity, by every means which God has put in his power, to resist and oppose the execution of it; that for us we will be ready to oppose it with our lives and fortunes. And the better to enable us to accomplish it, we will immediately form ourselves into a military body, to consist of companies to be made up out of the several townships under the following association, which is declared to be the Association of Westmoreland County.' "

Photography by Robert D. Shangle

A reconstructed soldier's barracks at Valley Forge National Historical Park, Valley Forge, Southeast Pennsylvania

Typical of the barracks for the soldier of the Continental Army, small huts were quickly constructed after arriving on December 19, 1777. The huts offered protection from miserably cold and snowy weather during the winter months of their occupation at Valley Forge.The soldiers suffered and existed on substandard rations, when available. "About 800 soldiers served in each of the sixteen brigades at Valley Forge. An estimated 34,577 pounds of meat and 168 barrels of flour per day were needed to feed the army. Soldiers relied on their home states or the Continental Congress to supply food, clothing and equipment. Shortages varied widely between the regiments. Any number of misfortunes — spoilage, bad roads, or capture by British foragers — could prevent supplies from reaching camp. General [Anthony] Wayne used troops and went to New Jersey to commandeer food when shortages occurred. Owners concealed their animals in the pine woods. He was so successful at obtaining supplies that he became known as The Drover."(*National Park Service*). General Washington stayed at Valley Forge until June 19, 1778.

Photography by Shangle Photographics

Memorial Square in Chambersburg, Franklin County, South-central Pennsylvania

Memorial Square, first known as The Diamond, has been a focal point in Chambersburg since before the Civil War. The fountain was added to the Square in 1878 as a memorial to Franklin County soldiers. Following a refurbishing in 1994, Memorial Square honors all American soldiers. Confederate soldiers occupied the town three different times during the war, finally burning a large portion of the city when the citizens refused to pay what the southern forces considered retribution money for damage done by the Union forces in the Shenandoah Valley. Earlier history was created by the presence of John Brown, who maintained a residence in Chambersburg preceding his famous unsuccessful raid on Harpers Ferry on October 16, 1859, on his quest to abolish slavery.

Photography by Robert D. Shangle

First Bank of the United States, Independence Square, Philadelphia

Created with the idea of unifying the nation's currency following the Revolutionary War, the First Bank of the United States was established to help solve the debt problem created by the war. There was heated debate regarding the involvement of the U. S. Congress participating in private business such as a bank, being in direct competition with state banks. At the time, each state had its own form of currency, and Lieutenant-Colonel Alexander Hamilton, aide to General Washington, suggested the creation of a standard form of currency among the states and encouraged the formation of a central bank to aid in the solution of the gigantic war debt and to support the much needed commerce within the nation. The bank, chartered in 1791, first occupied Carpenter's Hall in Philadelphia. By 1795 the First Bank building was being constructed with completion in 1797, costing a total amount of $110,168.05. The bank's presence ended in 1811 when Congress no longer supported the charter. The structure now ranks as the oldest bank building in America. Shipping magnate Stephen Girard purchased the bank and created the Stephen Girard Bank. The Girard National Bank occupied the building until 1926. It is now maintained by the National Park Service and is not open to the public.

Photography by Shangle Photographic

Longwood Gardens, Kennett Square, Southwest of Philadelphia

Pierre du Pont, the great grandson of Eleuthére Irénée du Pont, bequeathed a gift of his house, gardens and surrounding grounds to the people "for the sole use of the public for purposes of exhibition, instruction, education and enjoyment." Since 1906 when Pierre du Pont purchased the land, he began his work at producing one of the finest gardens in the world. The refinement of the gardens are many within the confines of the area. The 600-foot long Flower Garden Walk was the first garden developed by du Pont, completed in 1907. The Conservatory was added in 1921, complete with music furnished by a grand pipe organ. Such areas as the Rose Garden, a Desert House, waterlily pools, the Palm House, and East Conservatory give pause to the visitor who appreciates the aesthetic grandness emulating throughout the entire complex. Creative achievements are displayed in the Theatre Garden, the Wisteria Garden, and the Peony Garden, and many other delightful spaces. All things change at Longwood Gardens, as with the seasonal presentations of floral and greenery designs; entertainment events; the spectacular Winter Fun Days, the Open Air Concerts, Theater productions, and the magnificent Christmas exhibit. Fountains and lights were always a favorite of Pierre du Pont, and he was a master in adapting them to the finest degree. Longwood Gardens is managed and maintained by the Longwood Foundation, established in 1937, seventeen years before du Pont's death in 1954 at the age of 84.
Photography by Shangle Photographics

The State Capitol in the city of Harrisburg, South-central Pennsylvania

Architect Joseph Huston had a "vision for the Pennsylvania State Capitol [which] was to create, from the great artistic heritage of the Italian Renaissance, a 'Palace of Art' that would stand as a monument to the new Renaissance in America." (*cpc.leg.state.pa.us/history*) He achieved that goal in 1906. Quality art by eminent artists of the day have achieved to "glorify Pennsylvania's achievements in labor, industry and history." The 14-foot 6-inch bronze and gilded statue of *Commonwealth* rises 272 feet above ground level, placed originally on the dome in 1905.

Photography by Shangle Photographics

Fort Pitt Blockhouse at Point State Park, Pittsburgh

Built between 1759 and 1761 by British soldiers, Fort Pitt was constructed for protection against the marauding Indians and the fighting French who were determined to rid the area of the Red Coats. The five-sided Blockhouse was located outside the walls of the main fort. The French had established Fort Duquesne on the same spot earlier, determined to hold on to and establish a French dominance on the North American continent. Today, the Blockhouse is the only remaining structure of the original fort, having the position as the oldest building in Pittsburgh. The fort was named for British Prime Minister, William Pitt.

Photography by Shangle Photographics

The Amish Family Garden near Lancaster, Southeast Pennsylvania

"Woman's work is never done," so it is often spoken, and it applies to the small family garden. Mother and daughter guide their horse through the fine raked ground, perhaps preparing for winter or a second crop of some fast growing vegetable. The colorful gourds, pumpkins and squash are collecting for future use for the family meals. Brilliant flowers used to edge the vegetables in the garden, often times attracting the always needed pollinating insects, so necessary for productive gardens. They are also offensive to some garden predators, helping to maintain an equal balance to productivity. Beyond the garden plot is the industrial corn field, where the field corn will stand in the sugar producing sun and wait for the proper amount of time for drying, then harvesting, all accomplished with the aid of the horse, perhaps several, a wagon and old-fashioned manpower. Pledged to a way of life separate from the materialistic one offered by the tall electric power lines found in the distance, the Amish farmer produces abundant crops in well groomed fields.

Photography by James Blank

Old Main at Pennsylvania State University, University Park Campus, State College, Central Pennsylvania

Easily recognized by the title Penn State, the university claims 1863 as the year when all things began for the school. The University states that "The original Old Main, built between 1857 and 1863, had grown unsafe to occupy by the early 1920s. It was razed in 1929 and rebuilt between 1929 and 1930. Above the columns are words from the July 2, 1862 Act of Congress signed by Abraham Lincoln: 'To promote liberal and practical education in the several pursuits and professions of life.' This is followed by words from the April 1, 1863 Act of the State Legislature: 'And the Faith of the state hereby pledged to carry the same into effect.' " Eleven men comprised the first graduating class, receiving degrees identified as Bachelor of Scientific Agriculture. In 1871 six women were admitted as students, the first graduating in 1873. The growth of Penn State has been robust and has spread to what the University describes as "Penn State's new World Campus, which 'graduated' its first student in 2000, uses the Internet and other new technologies to offer instruction on an 'anywhere, anytime' basis." (*http://www.psu.edu/*). Today there are twenty-four campus locations statewide and over 80,000 students. University Park Campus is home to some 40,000 students.
Photography by Robert D. Shangle

The Herr Mill at Mill Bridge Village, Strasburg, Southeast Pennsylvania

The Mill Bridge Village states that it is "The oldest continuously operated historic village in the Pennsylvania Dutch Country." A visit to the village will attest to that statement. The 1728 mill, built by John Herr and known as Herr's Grist Mill, is still a gathering place, just as it was in colonial times when grain was ground into flour for the local patrons. Nearby is the local blacksmith, the much needed broommaker of the day, and the Amish House and Quilt Loft. Visitors can tour the grounds while enjoying a horse-drawn buggy ride, which passes through the historic 180-foot Herr's Mill Bridge.

Photography by James Blank

Historic St. Peter's Episcopal Church and churchyard, Philadelphia

Wander through the churchyard and view the old dates recorded on the headstones. It is an introduction to a marvelous history class. The remains of John Nixon, founder of St. Peter's Episcopal Church back in September, 1761, was laid to rest here. On July 8, 1776, he gave the first public reading of the Declaration of Independence. St. Peter's Church states there are eight Indian Chiefs buried in the cemetery, who died following an epidemic of small pox in 1793. An active congregation beckons to all visitors and would-be parishioners to its historical body, where little has changed in appearance over these many years.

Photography by James Blank

The city of Bellefonte, Central Pennsylvania

The French statesman, Charles Maurice de Talleyrand (1754-1838) is given the honor for the name of this center of historical architecture. The story dictates that he was so inspired when he viewed the abundant spring that provides some 13.5-million gallons of water daily, he exclaimed *La belle Fontaine.* James Dunlop acquired the land from William Lamb in 1794, and he and his son platted the town that grew to be one of the most influential cities" between Pittsburgh and Harrisburg. It spawned one eminent political figure after another, boasted a half-dozen opera houses, and at one point supported two daily and five weekly newspapers." (*http://bellefonte.org*) The Historic District in Bellefonte is extensive, and many homes are available for tours.

Photography by Robert D. Shangle

Mount Washington Tavern, Fort Necessity National Battleground, east of Uniontown, Southwest Pennsylvania

The tavern was completed in 1828 by Judge Nathaniel Ewing, owner of the Great Meadow that had been the site of the Battle of Fort Necessity on July 3, 1754. George Washington purchased the land in about 1769, maintaining ownership until his death in 1799. The tavern acquired its name from George Washington's historic presence. "Begun in 1811, the National Road was America's first Federally funded highway and the first step in the development of a national road system. It ran from Cumberland, Md. to Vandalia, Ill. with a substantial section in southwestern Pennsylvania." (*National Park Service*) By the time the tavern was built along the National Road, traffic was constant, and it continued until the mid-1850s. Mount Washington Tavern was considered a stagecoach stop, compared to a wagon stand. The accommodations were more refined at the stagecoach tavern. Food, drink, and lodging were offered at all taverns. Sleeping facilities were not exactly private; more so if the available bed was in a separate room as opposed to being in the upper loft where rows of beds were available. Sleeping partners could change during the night, sometimes more than once, depending upon the travel times of the stranger you "bunked" with. Food was robust, as was the available drink. As the railroad pushed across the country, the National Road was less traveled. With the advent of the automobile, highway travel again became popular. Soon the National Road was designated U.S. Highway 40. The Mount Washington Tavern has been renovated and redecorated to the period of activity in the 1800s. Tours are available, illustrating the typical accommodation afforded weary travelers.

Photography by Robert D. Shangle

The Golden Plough Tavern and the General Horatio Gates House, York, Southeast Pennsylvania

If the walls of the two oldest buildings in York could talk, visitors would be giddy knowing the "real insight" to the goings-on during the nation's formative years. Some folks at this time were beginning to refer to this new country as the United States of America. The Golden Plough Tavern was built in 1741, with the first known tavern license issued in 1753 to Martin Eichelberger. The "substantial dwelling house" of stone and brick was built between 1751 and 1754, being rented by one General Horatio Gates in 1778, from January to April during the time the Continental Congress was in session in York. The city of York is a history lesson waiting to be absorbed. The National Register of Historic Preservation recognizes more than half of the city's building as designated historic sites. The York County Heritage Trust, along with the Visitors Bureau, and the City of York maintain a most informative center perfect for historic browsing and exchanging questions for answers.

Photography by Robert D. Shangle

Drake Well at Drake Well Museum, Titusville, Northwest Pennsylvania

Colonel Edwin L. Drake discovered oil at Titusville on August 28, 1859. Oil became evident at a depth of 69.5 feet, giving rise to one of the biggest industries in Pennsylvania. Soon oil wells appeared all over the upper western region of the state, and the flow from them was enough for Pennsylvania to have produced sixty percent of the nation's oil through the turn of the century. A real hands-on experience is available at the Drake Well Museum, the site where Edwin Drake drilled the world's first oil well. The constant sound of a true oil operation is ongoing at the museum. A replica of the original well is here and the museum states that the "Outdoor exhibits of oil field machinery in our 210-acre park setting along Oil Creek includes a working central power lease with rodlines and pumping jacks, a 100 [year] old pumping station, and an early steel drilling rig."

Photography by Robert D. Shangle

General Lee's Headquarters Museum, Gettysburg, Southeast Pennsylvania

General Robert E. Lee needed a safe, strong building to live in during the Battle of Gettysburg and he chose the house occupied by Mrs. Mary Thompson. The thick stone walls afforded protection to the General and to his headquarters; also to Mrs. Thompson and her family during the deluge of battle that took place from July 1 to July 4, 1763. The house became a museum in 1922, displaying artifacts and pertinent material identified with the Civil War battle. "It was in this house that great men of history pondered the problems before them and made plans for one of the greatest battles of all times. The battle of Gettysburg lasted three days but the memories of this historical event are preserved to this day in this building, the Gettysburg headquarters of General Robert E. Lee." (*www.civilwarheadquarters.com*)
Photography by James Blank

Carpenters' Hall, Independence National Historical Park, Philadelphia, Southeast Pennsylvania

A building long remembered as the "Birthplace of a Nation" is Carpenters' Hall, completed in 1774, just in time to house one of the most important meetings in America's history. The National Park Service best explains: "When the First Continental Congress met to decide ways of recovering certain colonial rights and liberties violated by various acts of the British government, Philadelphia was the logical choice for the meeting. The principal city of the Colonies, it offered not only all the amenities the delegates needed but also a central location between North and South, a major consideration in an era of slow, tedious, and sometimes dangerous travel. . . . The Congress convened at Carpenters' Hall in September 1774 and addressed a declaration of rights and grievances to King George III. The delegates also agreed to boycott English goods and resolved that, unless their grievances were redressed, a second Congress should assemble the following spring. England did nothing to satisfy American complaints . . . . " The Carpenters' Company was organized to share information about the art of building, determine the value of completed work, hone architectural skills, and help indigent craftsmen. . . . [It is] the oldest trade guild in the country." (*www.ushistory.org*) Carpenters' Hall served as the headquarters for the First Bank of the United States in 1791. A nostalgic visit to the Hall allows a step back into history, with the ability to step "in their footsteps," view original furniture, and visit with an informative guide. The Carpenters' Company still own and operate the hall, a vital part of American heritage.

Photography by James Blank

Knox Bridge, within Valley Forge National Historical Park, Valley Forge, Southeast Pennsylvania

Built in 1865, eighty-seven years after the famous encampment by troops of the Continental Army at Valley Forge, a covered bridge was built over Valley Creek, up river from the iron forge built in 1740 that gave the location its name. Two rather famous people lived in the area who had the sir-name of Knox: General Henry Knox, who served General George Washington during the Valley Forge winter encampment and who proved to be one of the most honorable of men throughout his military career; Philander Knox, a high spirited attorney who served as U. S. Attorney General during President William McKinley's administration and who was Secretary of State during President William Howard Taft's administration. Which Knox the bridge is named for is not certain. The bridge, sixty-five feet long and thirteen feet wide, is also referred to the Valley Forge Bridge.

Photography by Shangle Photographics

Bridal Veil Falls along Pond Run Creek in the Pocono Mountains, Northeast Pennsylvania

The misty, spring-fed, cascading waters of Bridal Veil Falls join the stream water of Pond Run on its way to the Little Bushkill River and the Delaware River. As one of three cascading falls along this stretch of Pond Run, Bridal Veil is in the middle position, flanked by the Bridesmaid's Falls. East of Stroudsburg along U. S. Highway 209 and north a short distance from Bushkill, the area is on the southern and western portion of the Delaware Water Gap National Recreation Area. Nearby on Little Bushkill River is the popular and picturesque Bushkill Falls, dropping 100 feet, just one of eight waterfalls in a forested and scenic gorge.

Photography by Shangle Photographics

The Second Bank of the United States/Portrait Gallery, National Historical Park, Philadelphia

First a bank and now an art gallery. Not just any bank but one that was sanctioned by President James Madison in 1816. Following the War of 1812, debt was excessive and the nation needed to pull itself out of the mire created by that war and debt. The charter lasted for twenty years, many of those years in a tumultuous struggle between the President of the United States, Andrew Jackson, and the president of the bank, Nicholas Biddle. There was a faction that believed the United States should not be in the banking business. A rhetorical battle took place between the President's supporters and Nicholas Biddle and his advocates who supported the bank. Jackson won the battle when he vetoed the continuation of the bank charter in 1832. The bank's doors were finally closed in 1836. The magnificent building, built between 1818 and 1824, was designed with the Greek Parthenon in mind, and it illustrates the finest of Greek architecture. The continuation of the building's use is now demonstrated by the current occupant, the Portrait Gallery, which displays portraits of the people who were in command during the 18th century. "Inside the barrel-vaulted structure, graceful Ionic columns compliment the portraits of revolutionary heroes and Federal statesman. Those painted represent a Who's Who of the 18th century. There are signers of the Declaration and Constitution in addition to military men and foreign emissaries." (*www.ushistory.org*) Works by such artists as Charles Willson Peale, James Sharples, and Thomas Sully hang in the Portrait Gallery.

Photography by Shangle Photographics

The city of Philadelphia and the University of Pennsylvania along the Schuylkill *(school kill)* **River**

It seems that Philadelphia has always been here, but not true. However, it claims roots that extend back to the 1640s, and that is old enough (just about) to say "always been here." William Penn founded the city in 1682 after having received ownership to the land from King Charles II of England, as a payment for a debt owed to his deceased father. Penn named the land Pennsylvania, honoring his father, Admiral Sir William Penn. The University of Pennsylvania, a sage institution, was founded in 1740 by Benjamin Franklin. Just two miles from downtown Philadelphia, the 260-acre campus is home to the first schools in Medicine, Law and Business.

Photography by James Blank

The Susquehanna River, Central Pennsylvania

Two arms of the Susquehanna River, the West Branch and the North Branch, sweep through west-central and northern Pennsylvania. They combine at Northumberland and Sunbury to form the main stem that winds through Pennsylvania. "The Susquehanna River, sixteenth largest river in America, is the largest river lying entirely in the United States that flows into the Atlantic Ocean. The Susquehanna and its hundreds of tributaries drain 27,500 square miles, an area nearly the size of South Carolina, spread over parts of New York, Pennsylvania, and Maryland. The river meanders 444 miles from its origin at Otsego Lake near Cooperstown, New York until it empties into the Chesapeake Bay at Havre de Grace, Maryland. The Susquehanna is the 'mother' river to the Chesapeake, providing 50 percent of all the freshwater entering the great estuary." (*sites.state.pa.us/PA*)

Photography by Shangle Photographics

The Strasburg Railroad, Strasburg, Southeast Pennsylvania

A trip through Lancaster County aboard the Strasburg Railroad is a relaxing way to experience true Amish Country. This is the heart of the Pennsylvania Dutch Country, where the Amish, Mennonite, and Dunkard people reside. The Strasburg Railroad train is powered by old-fashioned steam-driven locomotives. The railroad was chartered on June 9, 1832, and has been operating as "America's oldest short line railroad," providing passenger service as well as freight service to the community. It provides a vital link to the nation's rail system. There are several-styled passenger cars that enhance an already exciting trip on the Strasburg, such as the Victorian parlor car — luxurious and full of splendor; the open-aired observation car that allows a "fresh air" closeness to the countryside; and the wooden coach that illustrates the utilitarian amenities to a train ride. The gently rolling countryside is dotted with Amish farms that display well maintained grounds, vibrant gardens, and acres of fields that yield abundant crops. The nearby town of Strasburg moves at a gentle pace, much as it has for the many years of its existence, frequented by the Amish horse-drawn buggy. Not far is the Mennonite Museum that provides much information about the area.
Photography by James Blank

The Youghiogheny River at Ohiopyle State Park, east of Uniontown, Southwest Pennsylvania

A recreational wonderment is Ohiopyle State Park. The Department of Conservation and Natural Resources describes it the best. "Located primarily in Fayette County, Ohiopyle State Park encompasses approximately 19,052 acres of rugged natural beauty and serves as the gateway to the Laurel Mountains. . . .The focal point of the area is the more than 14 miles of the Youghiogheny [yaw-ki-gay-nee] River Gorge that passes through the heart of the park. The 'Yough' [yawk] provides some of the best whitewater boating in the Eastern U.S. as well as spectacular scenery. . . . Old records indicate that the name of Ohiopyle was derived from the American Indian word 'Ohiopehhle' which means 'white frothy water,' a reference to the large falls on the Youghiogheny River. . . . In 1754, George Washington was trying to find a water supply route for his attempt to capture Fort Duquesne, now Pittsburgh. When Washington got to the falls he abandoned his plans to use the Youghiogheny River."

Photography by Shangle Photographics

61

Wheatland, home to President James Buchanan, Lancaster, Southeast Pennsylvania

President James Buchanan can well be remembered as a Pennsylvanian who made his home state proud. President Buchanan served his country during one of the most tumultuous periods in the nation's history, the time immediately preceding the Civil War, when the country was being pulled apart due to the slavery issue. When he turned the reins of power over to Abraham Lincoln, he is quoted to state: "If you are as happy, my dear sir, on entering this house as I am in leaving it and returning home, you are the happiest man in this country." President Buchanan retired to his home, Wheatland, in Lancaster, purchased from William Jenkins in 1848 and who gave the house the title because of the bountiful wheatfields that surrounded the property. Buchanan served his country well. Following his short but illustrious stint as an attorney in Lancaster, Buchanan was elected state representative at the age of twenty-three, serving two terms. He moved on to a position as a U. S. Congressman, serving for ten years; then he became the Minister to Russia in 1832. In 1834 he was elected to the U. S. Senate, representing Pennsylvania until 1845, leaving to serve his president, James Knox Polk, as Secretary of State. James Buchanan became the 15th President of the United States on March 4, 1857, and he served until March 3, 1861. He carries the distinction of being the only bachelor president in our nation's history. He was engaged to Miss Ann Coleman, but their relationship was severed following a quarrel. She died soon after, devastating the young Buchanan. James Buchanan was born, some say, on April 23, 1791, in Mercersburg, Pennsylvania and died at Wheatland on June 1, 1868. He is buried in Woodward Hill Cemetery in Lancaster.
Photography by Shangle Photographics

The Liberty Bell, located within the Liberty Bell Pavilion on Market Street, Philadelphia

Each person reading the inscription of the Liberty Bell interprets the words to his own needs: *Proclaim LIBERTY throughout all the Land unto all the inhabitants thereof* (*Leviticus 25:10*). "In 1751, the Speaker of the Pennsylvania Assembly ordered a new bell for the State House. He asked that a Bible verse to [sic] be placed on the bell. . . . As the official bell of the Pennsylvania State House (today called Independence Hall) it rang many times for public announcements, but we remember times like July 8, 1776 when it rang to announce the first public reading of the Declaration of Independence." The first bell that arrived in Philadelphia cracked and was replaced by a second bell in 1753. "By 1846 a thin crack began to affect the sound of the [new] bell. The bell was repaired in 1846 and rang for a George Washington birthday celebration, but the bell cracked again and has not been rung since. No one knows why the bell cracked either time. . . . The bell weighs about 2000 pounds. It is made of 70% copper, 25% tin, and small amounts of lead, zinc, arsenic, gold, and silver. It hangs from what is believed to be its original yoke, made from American elm, also known as slippery elm." (*National Park Service: www.nps.gov*)

Photography by Courtesy of Independence National Historic Park

The Cathedral of Learning, on the campus of the University of Pittsburgh, Western Pennsylvania

Chancellor John Gabbert Bowman faced the challenge of providing for the welfare of the students at the University of Pittsburgh when he became the tenth chancellor in 1921. Space on the campus grounds was minimal, and he believed that the answer to the problem was to "go up" and erect a tall building that would take up a small amount of ground. "The building was to be more than a schoolhouse; it was to be a symbol of the life that Pittsburgh through the years had wanted to live. It was to make visible something of the spirit that was in the hearts of pioneers as, long ago, they sat in their log cabins and thought by candlelight of the great city that would be sometimes spread out beyond their three rivers that even they were starting to build." (*Quote by John Gabbert Bowman*). He expressed these words to demonstrate the need for what became known as the Cathedral of Learning, a 42-story Gothic stone building, believed to be the tallest academic building in the Western Hemisphere.

Photography by Robert D. Shangle

providing access to recreation sites. Warren, one of Pennsylvania's bigger oil towns, is on its northern perimeter by the Allegheny River, which winds along the northern and western forest border. Kane is a community located on the eastern edge of the forest, at an elevation of 2,013 feet above sea level. Pittsburgh-area ski tourists come here to take advantage of its early snows.

Up in Pennsylvania's sawed-off northwestern panhandle is the Lake Erie plain, with gently rolling farmland that ends at the lake's shores. The city of Erie sits on these shores and keeps healthy from the heavy lake traffic into and out of its ports. Erie is a busy shipping and industrial town, but manages at the same time to maintain the serene look of a resort center. Its prime physical traits are spaciousness and generally low roof lines, even in its downtown district. It was planned along the lines of the national capital; it preserves those lines even more fully than modern Washington, D.C. does. It has great historic importance too, in keeping with the Keystone State's crucial role in our early history. Commodore Oliver Hazard Perry launched his victorious encounter with British warships in Lake Erie during the War of 1812 from Presque Isle Peninsula. Known as the Battle of Lake Erie, Perry, at the age of twenty-eight, orchestrated the successful battle, opening the door to a successful campaign for the final defeat of the British. He is well remembered for the words he wrote to General William Henry Harrison when he stated, "We have met the enemy and they are ours . . . ."

The Pennsylvania Department of Conservation and Natural Resources states that "Presque Isle is a recurring sand spit jutting into Lake Erie and has the only surf beach in the Commonwealth." A French word meaning "almost an island," the peninsula curves out and around within Lake Erie, creating a nearly landlocked body of water known as Presque Isle Bay, fronting the city of Erie. As a state park, Presque Isle is seven miles long and is equipped with bathing beaches along Lake Erie, natural wooded areas for exploring, excellent picnic areas, and marvelous hiking and skating pathways.

The handsome Erie Maritime Museum that opened in 1998 is home port for the reconstructed *U. S. Brig Niagara*, the ship Commodore Perry boarded when his own vessel, the flagship *Lawrence*, was damaged during the eventful battle. The hull of the *Niagara* was raised in 1913 from the watery depths of Misery Bay in Lake Erie where it had been scuttled in 1820. It was restored and displayed, honoring the ship at a centennial tribute of the Battle of Lake Erie. But beginning in 1987, a massive renovation took place, restoring the vessel to the finest of conditions, declaring the ship to be the Official Flagship of the Commonwealth of Pennsylvania. The city of Erie has been declared the Flagship City as well. The ship is available for tours and sailing excursions. The Erie Maritime Museum and the *Niagara* are focal points within the city and a must-see item for a truly hands-on experience of Erie's maritime history, which includes exhibits of reconstructed sections of Perry's first flagship, the *Lawrence*, and much more. The museum is located just east of Dobbins Landing where the Bicentennial Tower is located, provided with two observation decks that allow an excellent opportunity to view Lake Erie and other significant sights of Erie.

It has been stated that the city of Pittsburgh is the beginning and the end of all that happens in western Pennsylvania. Whether this is true, to such an absolute degree, is a question best left unanswered. The city at the confluence of the three rivers, the Allegheny, Monongahela, and the Ohio, is indeed the centerpiece of a region that contains immense natural wealth and a large portion of rugged mountain and valley environment. Economically, geographically, and historically, Pittsburgh has been the fulcrum upon which everything else moves. Its vitality as a city has come from the great waves of ethnic groups flowing into it from other parts of this country and the world. The Germans, Lithuanians, Serbs, Hungarians, English, Scottish, Irish, Italians, and others of the United States have come together to create a city of great drive and enormous confidence in its abilities. Pittsburgh's people are proud of their city — they even used to brag about the smoke and grime of its industrial district. But that brag is almost passé, because Pittsburgh has cleaned and polished that industrial district. The converging Allegheny and Monongahela rivers form its famed Golden Triangle, a symbol of its industrial and financial might. Pittsburgh has come a long way since the French and British were scuffling over whose fort it was back in the 1750s.

Important Facts

State Name: *Pennsylvania*
William Penn named his domain to honor his father and for the sylvan area of the land, meaning wooded and rich with forest.

Nickname: *The Keystone State*
Refers to the final stone placed within an arch that holds the other stones in place and together.

Motto: *Virtue,*
Liberty, and
Independence

Firsts: To established the first public school in the American Colonies: 1698.

To establish the first medical school, 1765, now known as University of Pennsylvania.

To established the first public bank in the United States: 1780: The Pennsylvania Bank.

From the Piedmont
to the Poconos

The Delaware Valley, with Philadelphia as its hub, spreads over the southeast corner of Pennsylvania, taking in four counties that fan out from the city like spokes of a wheel. It is part of the state where a web of highways tie together a thicket of residential and industrial centers that make up one of the worlds biggest concentration of people. The Delaware river front, along most of its plain, has that man made look that large port facilities acquire in our day and age. Shipyards, steel mills, factories, oil refineries, and giant piers elbow each other for river bank space. Several million people have crowded together in this corner of the state, so it would seem unlikely that much open space would remain. Yet it does, in the big city itself, in the stylish and beautiful suburbs on the north and west, and in the far edges of the four surrounding counties, where the rolling Piedmont country begins.

The carefully preserved open spaces within this urban complex may, sometimes, owe their natural beauty to what happened there before we were yet a nation. Valley Forge is one of these places, both beautiful and sacred. Now a National Historic Park, the rolling valley has been frozen in time, much as it was during that heroic winter encampment of George Washington's patriot army in December of 1777. Now, as then, the snow sometimes comes in deep drifts during the winter, piling against today's replicas of the soldiers' crude log huts, as it did against the original barracks during that winter of hardship. Today, the campground is close by the bulging limits of Philadelphia's suburbs, but still aloof from the town where the British were so comfortably garrisoned, languishing in their glory of having defeated the Continental Army at Brandywine and Germantown. When it is not wintertime at Valley Forge, the outlook is green and glorious. The hills around are crowded with oaks and maples; around its northern perimeter flows the big Schuylkill River (pronounced school kil), now paralleled by the big, fast moving Schuylkill Expressway into Philadelphia.

Other reminders of the Revolution crowd into this corner of Pennsylvania. Southwest of Philadelphia some thirty miles is Brandywine Creek. Just before the stream enters the state of Delaware, on its way to the river of the same name, is the town of Chadds Ford, on the east bank. Here is where the Battle of Brandywine took place on September 11, 1777, when General George Washington and his outnumbered army tried unsuccessfully to prevent the British from taking Philadelphia. The Brandywine battle of today is more concerned with conservation than maneuvers. Its soft, rolling hills and the big, old maple and sycamore trees lining the now-diminished creek have been organized into the Brandywine Conservation Area, a managed mixture of contour farms and wildlife ponds.

Descendants of Eleuthére Irenée du Pont de Nemours, founder of the DuPont dynasty, have enriched the state of Pennsylvania with one of the world's most extensive botanical collections. Pierre du Pont, the great grandson of Eleuthére Irenée du Pont, bequeathed a gift of his house, gardens and surrounding grounds to the people "for the sole use of the public for purposes of exhibition, instruction, education and enjoyment." Since 1906 when Pierre du Pont purchased the land, he began his work at producing one of the finest gardens in the world. Longwood Gardens, located between Chadds Ford and Kennett Square southwest of Philadelphia, combines outdoor gardens, arboretums, fountains, and greenhouses with thousands of different kinds of exotic plants.

To the north of Philadelphia is another hallowed site like Valley Forge, Washington Crossing Historic Park, outside the village of Washington Crossing. The park commemorates the event involving General George Washington and his bedraggled, never-say-die army who made the crossing of the Delaware River on Christmas night, 1776. The success of that campaign became a turning point in the winning of the Revolutionary War. Washington and his men captured Trenton, New Jersy, from the Hessian troups (German mercenary troops fighting with the British). On the river bank where Washington actually embarked, now stand buildings preserved and restored from that long-ago time. The Thompson-Neeley House, once occupied by Revolutionary forces during the preparation for the river crossing, contains construction dating back to 1702. The McKonkey's Ferry Inn stands as a reminder of the days when the building was used "as a guard post" during the Continental Army's encampment in Bucks County in December, 1776 . . . . The *spiritof 76.com* states that "According to tradition this is where Washington and his aides ate their Christmas dinner prior to the historic crossing." There are several more historic buildings providing information regarding historic Bucks County. Visitors are drawn here all year round. At Christmas each year, a reenactment of the famous Crossing of the Delaware occurs, with actors in Colonial uniforms making the trip in a boat like that which was used by Washington and his troops.

The countryside from Philadelphia north toward Easton is a patchwork of mellow vistas that yield to no other part of the country for pure, shameless beauty. Bucks County, lying along the river on the north edge of the city, accomplishes all this by natural charm overlaid with an abundance of history. Washington Crossing is one of its special places. Another is New Hope, "the oldest town in Solebury township," located a few miles up the Delaware River. Records indicate that New Hope's history dates back to 1710 when William Penn granted land to Richard Heath and his heirs. The little colony of writers and artists, located in the wooded hills, dates from Revolutionary times and has a settled-in look that is reminiscent of European towns. Many of its old buildings have been converted to be used as shops and restaurants. The historic Delaware Canal glides through the town, reaching into upper Bucks County. The fifty-nine-mile-long canal opened for commercial navigation in 1834 and continued operating until 1931. The canal was a link in the water route from Lake Erie to the ports of Philadelphia and New York. Now it carries only visitors and sightseers along its placid green banks in barges pulled by mules plodding along the well-trod towpath. North of New Hope is a photogenic world of little valleys that drop steeply to dark and cool floors, where clear streams chatter briskly or softly murmur on their way to the Delaware River. Further inland, the countryside is dotted with villages where stone houses and whitewashed barns sit by rushing creeks in settings that evoke the spirit of past time.

Even the very heart of Philadelphia itself has its open space. The most noteworthy example of this is Fairmount Park, a huge reserve where William Penn's idea of a "Greene countrie towne" seems to be fulfilled. The park stretches for several miles over hills along both sides of the Schuykill River in west-center Philadelphia and for several more miles along Wissahickon Creek to the north. The park is maintained in as natural a state as possible. Its trees and dells, creeks and rocky outcroppings flank the river and creek with soul-restoring beauty in the midst of the city's tight concentrations of residential neighborhoods. Man made beauty finds a sanctuary in the park, too. A great number of statues and outdoor sculptures are found along the park drives. The Fairmount Park Commission governs the seven Fairmount Park Mansions. Each house is administered and maintained by a philanthropic organization. These elegant homes were once owned and occupied by prominent figures of the nation's early days. The houses were constructed in the mid- to late 1700s.

Most Americans know that Philadelphia's core area is filled with some of the nation's most sacred relics and hallowed buildings. The "old city" near the Delaware River is known as the Birthplace of the Nation, and rightfully so. Here, Independence National Historical Park provides a well groomed setting for some of our most famous old buildings, including, of course, Independence Hall. Nearby is Elfreth's Alley, just off Independence Park near the river in what is identified as Old City. The cobblestone street, looking like a setting for a Charles Dickens novel, is only six feet wide, with its thirty-three brick houses huddled against each other as if for support. The Elfreth's Alley Museum is but one of the houses opened to the public; most of the others are private residences, all dating back to the early 1700s. Elfreth's Alley is considered "the oldest street in the oldest part of Old City," dating back to 1702, and it is a National Historic Landmark. Fete Days are celebrated in June, a time when an historical excursion of the Alley is available, with period-costumed participants illustrating the goings-on of early Philadelphia. It is one of the ways Philadelphia remembers and honors its past, while making bold moves in the present time toward creating a better "Greene countrie towne."

Farther west in southeastern Pennsylvania is the stronghold of the world famous Pennsylvania Dutch. The "Dutch" are really German in origin, descendants of sectarian refugees from the Rhineland who came to William Penn's liberal lands in the early and middle 18th century to practice their religious beliefs and personal philosophies in peace. The Pennsylvania Dutch have established themselves in some of the world's best farming country. Regardless of their strict or not-so-strict beliefs and practices, they have been an extremely valuable and productive element in the life of the state and of the nation. Three Pennsylvania counties are best known as "Dutch" country: Berks, Lebanon, and Lancaster. Here the Germanic influence and traditions are best observed in the small villages, such as Millersville and Manheim, Ephrata, Hamburg, Kutztown, and Emmaus, even though the bigger "Dutch" towns like Lancaster, Lebanon, Reading, and Allentown have made more of a tourist attraction out of the Dutch culture.

Not only the eye but also the nose can appreciate the rich textures of the Dutch country. Undulating fields and aromatic barnyards are a sensory treat. Everything has a prosperous, well tended appearance, from the spacious, hipped-roof farm buildings to the neat fields and sleek livestock. The healthy looking farm families are their own advertisement for their prosperity. Sometimes the big barns of the "fancy farmer" have hex signs on them in a variety of colorful red, blue, yellow and white geometrical designs. The hex circles, created of geometric designs and placed on the barns to instill good luck, are more for decoration these days than anything else, but a little crop insurance does not hurt.

The most readily identifiable sect of all has a large representation in the Lancaster-Reading area. The strict observance of practices deriving from the sect's beginnings still is the rule in the daily lives of the Amish. The city of Lancaster has some farmers markets where the "Plain People," as they are called, come in their somber clothing to sell their produce, the women in their bonnets, the men with their beards and broad-brimmed hats. The farm crops will probably have arrived at the stalls by horse and buggy. Motorized conveniences are not part of the Amish life style. The very strictest families ban photographs, mirrors, and indoor plumbing as "vanities" not in accord with their religious beliefs.

While becoming settled by German refugees, this corner of Pennsylvania was also involved in the Revolution, and some artifacts of that time are still around. One of these is restored Hopewell Furnace, located outside of Elverson within French Creek State Park south of Reading. The forge and Revolutionary-era Hopewell Village have been restored and are listed as a National Historic Site. It was one of the suppliers of cannonballs to the Continental Army.

Nearby is the Daniel Boone Homestead, not far from French Creek Park. Daniel Boone was born here and his family homestead is preserved . Boone's father, a Quaker, is believed to have built part of the brownstone house in the 1730s. Squire and Sarah Morgan Boone, Daniel's parents, constructed a single room, one-story log house over a cellar and spring. Daniel was born in 1734, joining five other siblings, and was the sixth of eleven children.

Before the Hopewell people thought of cannonballs, and possibly before the elder Mr. Boone thought of Daniel, somebody unknown in the Conestoga Valley south of Lancaster invented a big, hefty wagon to take care of the growing freight needs of the Philadelphia-Lancaster link. The famed Conestoga wagon became the country's transportation of choice for more than a century, reincarnated as the prairie schooner later on when migration pushed out into the Far West.

Northeast Pennsylvania is a mountain-and-lake kingdom with a distinctly different "feel" from the high country in the central part of the state. These are the Poconos, lower than some of the more remote ridges around the state, and probably a tamer wilderness. Lakes are everywhere in these gentle elevations, adding a fresh, cool ingredient to the pine-scented Pocono air even on the hottest of days. Lately, the winter bird and wildlife of the Poconos have had to share their living quarters with people who have discovered that the slopes around here are just right for ski runs. These handy mountains have become a favorite recreational retreat for people from eastern Pennsylvania, northern New Jersey, and southern New York.

On the eastern limits of the Poconos flows the Delaware River, dividing Pennsylvania from the state of New Jersey and cutting through both states. Where the notch is made, the Delaware River has fashioned a majestic natural wonderland that is one of Pennsylvania's scenic masterpieces. The beautiful gorge is called the Delaware Water Gap National Recreation Area, slicing between two fault blocks at an elevation of 1,200 feet. The Appalachian Trail goes by here, high on the mountain shoulders. Pennsylvania and New Jersey share the nearly 70,000 acres of protected land that were set aside in 1965 "for public outdoor recreation use and for the preservation of scenic, scientific and recreation resources," so states the National Park Service. Park staff members provide educational programs and activities. A day or two of total adventure is available within the park by using the extensive scenic drives, biking and hiking trails through the hills, swimming in the Delaware River, and by taking time to view the wildlife and birds in their natural habitat.

A few miles away from the Gap is another of the state's old historic towns, Stroudsburg, built by Colonel Jacob Stroud, a veteran of the French and Indian War and which began as a stockade. Stroudsburg became a Moravian town (a Protestant religious group having roots to 1457) while serving as a haven for Revolutionary casualties. Its location amidst the Pocono-Kittatinny Mountains and valleys makes it especially attractive to visitors. In autumn the mountain slopes around it are ablaze with the russet tones of turning foliage.

Big Pocono State Park, a few miles to the west, is a good place to become acquainted with the fabulous old geology revealed on the rock walls of about every road-cut made in these mountains. Big Pocono is 2,131 feet in the air and located in the rugged terrain of Camelback Mountain. There are coral rock and marine fossils in these hills, proving that seas washed over the land in some impossibly ancient era. Probably some not-so-ancient glaciers crushed down from the north more than once. The lakes that show up everywhere are results of the glaciers, which carved out lakebeds as they retreated from a warming climate. Bruce Lake is one of these, a forty-eight acre jewel within a large natural area next to Promised Land State Park in the Poconos. The lake is unreachable by roads, and accessible only by hiking trail. One of the most enjoyable experiences, available from many high points along the Pocono and Kittatinny ridges, is the long view of myriad ranges and rolling hills to the far horizon. Three states come within the compass of the eye on the highest points, ever changing perspectives of the nearby Delaware Water Gap itself.

The Pocono playground is all the more remarkable for its nearness to the famed anthracite coal fields of the state. The Poconos——the mountains and plateau—practically skirt the big coal towns of Scranton and Wilkes-Barre, and the smaller ones like Carbondale and Honesdale. Yet their psychological distance from those nearby industrial areas on the west is immense; their gentle wilderness is quite a miraculous instance of beauty and utility existing compatibly in close proximity.

The Delaware River flows big and broad and businesslike past the industrial dock sides of lower Pennsylvania and New Jersey, but the upper river is another creature. As it begins to carve out that wriggled eastern border of the state, it is very much a sparkling mountain stream, casting glittery lights off of its blue waters. Sometimes it is a green river, reflecting the dense woods and shrubs of the bank side. Cutting through the long, green forested mountain ridges, the Delaware River pours over rocks and ledges and shows off its shallow bed through limpid waters. The plentiful fish attract fishing birds: herons, kingfishers, and mergansers. Along this narrow upper river, the natural scene is in charge, with little evidence of human activity. River-bank towns of this corner county (Wayne) are tiny and infrequent. The stretch of river that they sit on has been involved in the affairs of a nation for a long time, in peace and war. The French and Indian wars seesawed through these mountains and forests, and along this river. Some of these Wayne County communities were close to the action, and some of their citizens were involved on one side or the other of the skirmishes.

The estate of Gifford Pinchot, having served Pennsylvania as governor from 1923 to 1927 and again in 1931 to 1935, reminds Pennsylvanians of Pinchot's wide ranging conservation interests, both as governor and as Director of Forestry during the Theodore Roosevelt and William Howard Taft administrations. The estate known as Grey Towers is in Milford, a lower Pike County town in eastern Pennsylvania that hangs over the Delaware River on a bluff. The onetime home of Gifford Pinchot is now home to the Pinchot Institute for Conservation and listed as a National Historic Landmark.

Mountains
and a River

From the north border to the south border, central Pennsylvania is an Oz-like complication of mountainous ridges, rolling plateau, quicksilver streams, and one grand river that rolls through its heart like an artery that keeps things in good working order. The Susquehanna River is, indeed, the life blood of the rugged interior. Not navigable except by shallow draft vessels, it is nevertheless a big water carrier, a mile wide in its lower reaches around Harrisburg. Its beautiful Indian name is supposedly a comment on how it looks after a hard rain: its meaning is "muddy river." Countless "runs" or mountain creeks that pour down ridges, which the river twists around as it moves along the land, feed the Susquehanna River. One major tributary, the Juniata River, comes in from the west, north of Harrisburg.

Two arms of the Susquehanna, the West Branch and the North Branch, sweep through west-central and northern Pennsylvania. They combine at Northumberland and Sunbury to form the main stem that winds through Pennsylvania, eastern Maryland for a short stint, then out into the Chesapeake Bay. Ever since people began to live in what is now Pennsylvania, the river and its wide fertile valley have been a controlling factor in their lives. Some of the earliest settlers along the Susquehanna were the Susquehannocks, part of the so-called Iroquois confederated nations who take a stance of independence from, and indeed a hatred of, Iroquois rule. They settled on the lower portion of the river, spreading out as far south as the Chesapeake Bay area. Until the latter part of the 17th century, they had defeated all Iroquois efforts to subdue them. But they gradually succumbed to Iroquois raids and the pressure of encroaching settlers along the West Branch, where they had retreated in the 1760s. Their numbers diminished until they were extinguished as a separate Indian tribe.

Early fur trappers were the first Europeans in the Susquehanna Valley. After William Penn received his charter for Pennsylvania in 1681, setters began arriving in the new colony in large numbers. By the mid-eighteenth century, they had spread to the lower Susquehanna and up along the main river to Shamokin (now Sunbury). As the century entered its second half, the North Branch of the upper river began to acquire both Pennsylvania and Connecticut settlers. The Wyoming Valley along the river was an area of conflict between the two groups. The Yankee invaders began farming the fertile soil but were forced by Pennsylvania troops on five separate occasions to retire to their rocky home colony. Some of the encounters were marked by great bloodshed. They lasted through the Revolution and into the 1780s. The famous Wyoming Massacre occurred during the Revolutionary period, when most of the Yankee settlements in the valley were destroyed by a New York alliance of British and Indians, and their inhabitants killed or captured.

The Wyoming Valley has been known both as the Great Warrior Path and Sullivan's Trail. The latter name came about due to a successful punitive expedition carried out by General John Sullivan, under the command of General George Washington, against the British and Iroquois involved in the Wyoming Massacre. Today, the North

Branch of the Susquehanna, curving in a giant arch as it comes south from New York past Scranton and Wilkes-Barre, has been designated a federal "scenic river."

Harrisburg, on the east bank of the Susquehanna's main stem at the edge of the mountain country, was "launched," one might say, as a ferry stop and trading post much earlier in the 18th century. The town, itself, was not established until 1785, by the son of the original founder of the post and named for him. Harrisburg's strategic position and its magnificent Susquehanna location brought it into contention for selection in 1789 as the new nation's capital city. The national congress in that year finally chose Washington, D. C. on the Potomac River. Harrisburg became Pennsylvania's capital in 1812.

When Harris' Ferry was laid out as a town, the state legislature made it the county seat of Dauphin County, the latter name reflecting the influence of French immigration during the French Revolution. The legislature then named the town Louisbourg, after Louis XVI. But John Harris, Jr., rose up in righteous wrath and refused to sell any more of his land for a town "except in Harrisburg." His ultimatum changed the legislative mind. The Harris family name was restored to the town and has remained. What has also remained is Harrisburg's great good looks, a combination of natural gifts and careful planning. The city's broad river drive lined with big old trees and magnificent homes gives it a regal dignity. The final touch is the ornate Italian Renaissance capitol, its dome rising majestically from the high perspective of hills back of the river. Harrisburg was and is a quiet place. It partakes of the Pennsylvania Dutch home-loving state of mind. The fair city's peace has only once been in danger of being interrupted and her noble vistas threatened. That was during the Civil War when Robert E. Lee's Confederate armies reached the outskirts, only to turn south to Gettysburg, where the climactic battle of the war was fought.

Gettysburg is across the river, in the history-laden countryside of south-central Pennsylvania. The "Dutch" are well represented here, too, in the York and Hanover precincts. York, founded in 1741, was the first settlement west of the Susquehanna River. It was the home of the Continental Congress during the British occupation of Philadelphia after the Brandywine campaign. A century later Gettysburg became the scene of another war in these southern Pennsylvania foothills. The area's serene beauty today makes all the more poignant its role in one of the Civil War's most terrible battles. Several million visitors each year come to Gettysburg's wood studded vales and wander over the battlefield and the hallowed ground of the National Military Park. At the Visitor Center a dialogue is heard about the incredible struggle that took place on July 1, 2, and 3, 1863, when the fortunes of the Union and the Confederacy hung in the balance. For over 51,000 men, Gettysburg was the place where many of them were killed and many of them received wounds that maimed them for life. Some 1,400 monuments studding the battlefield's 6,000 rolling acres contribute powerfully toward a feeling for what happened there. In the National Cemetery of the battlefield park, the Soldier's National Monument marks the site of some brief remarks by Abraham Lincoln at the dedication ceremonies. Of all the marvelously wrought monuments dedicated to those who fought there, the most complete and perfect is that short two-minute speech — the Gettysburg Address.

South-central Pennsylvania is in the thick of the mountain march through the state. The ridges of the Tuscarora and Blue mountains stretch for many miles like giant waves following one upon the other. In long vista views across blue-green valleys, the land merges with a hazy-purple horizon. Cowans Gap State Park, in heavily forested mountains, is profuse with wildflowers at certain times of the year. The little, sheltered mountain valleys sometimes have a story to tell that goes hand-in-hand with the scenery. Samuel Cowan, a young British officer, and his bride from Boston, homesteaded more than two-hundred years ago at what became known as Cowans

Gap. She remained in this bird- and flower- filled, creek-watered spot long after her husband's death, being discovered living in her home at the age of 102 by a surveying party.

The West Branch is the less settled arm of the Susquehanna River. It cuts into the heart of the Allegheny Mountains from a beginning far into the western side of the Pennsylvania rectangle. Unlike the North Branch, much of its course is through deep wilderness. Its valley is very much small town territory, with communities exceeding two-hundred years of existence. This is central Pennsylvania, another distinct part of the state. Its big towns are Williamsport, an historic old community and former lumber center on the West Branch; Sunbury, where the West and North branches join together; State College in Centre County. The city of Lewistown is on the Juniata River, a gorgeous stream that cuts through some of the complicated ridges between here and Mifflintown, forming a four-mile-long wooded gorge called the Lewistown Narrows.

The "Dutch" are found here, too. Their presence is felt in the look of the small towns, in the look of the people, and in the rich agricultural lands outside of the towns. Although this mountainous region is less fertile than the rich limestone hills around Lancaster and Lebanon, there is still a lot of farming that gets done. In this part of Pennsylvania, where the broken terrain seems almost independent of the ruling stream that is the upper West Branch, the towns are minor interruptions in the midst of rolling fields of corn and wheat. The forests seem to be everywhere else, wherever a slope begins to rise into the wall of surrounding ridges. Forest grows along spanning highways that lead to the towns, which transform the area. The houses, some with clapboard siding and others made of brick or stone, snuggle close to the street, with wide porches running along the front and sometimes around the sides of the houses. Mellow red brick churches and unobtrusive shops are found in the core areas. The sidewalks are narrow and the main street through town curves and dips to follow the rolling landscape. They are friendly places.

Central Pennsylvania offers great adventure to the visitor of its mountains and valleys. That initial excitement is experienced when the first range of mountains shows up across the river from Harrisburg.

Going up the east bank north of the city, the highway passes Rockville Bridge, carrying the Pennsylvania Railroad tracks across the Susquehanna River. Twelve miles north of Harrisburg is Clark's Ferry then on to Amity Hall, located on the west side of the Susquehanna. Amity Hall was once important as the intersection point of Pennsylvania's east-west and north-south canal systems. Now Amity Hall is a popular stop for highway travelers. North is Girty's Face, a natural cliff formation along the road side, looking like the long nosed face of a man. The cliff has been traditionally known as Girty's Face, named for Simon Girty, a renegade Revolutionary soldier who joined up with the Indians and supposedly hid himself in a nearby mountain cave.

U. S. Highway 15 continues north along the west side of the Susquehanna River through such towns as Liverpool, across the river from Millersburg, Port Trevorton, leading to Lewisburg. The river route may be abandoned here for State Highway 45 that cuts cross country in a westerly direction. From the tiny village of Hartleton, the road lifts a long incline grade into Bald Eagle State Forest, high on Paddy Mountain. This route through dense forest is called the Seven-Mile Narrows, and leads through some of Pennsylvania's wildest and most spectacular forest and mountain country. You can almost become intoxicated by the incredible pine woods fragrance, almost as thick as syrup as it hangs in the air.

The eyes get a workout, too, gazing at the abundant dark green forest that stretches endlessly back from the road. The Narrows is rather like a roller coaster, a curving, up-and-down defile through the mountain. This wilderness area shelters an abundance of wildlife, from deer to raccoon, bear, fox, beaver, and wildcat. (Pennsylvania harbors more wild animals than any other northeastern state. A great deal of the animals roam these high ridges and deep valleys of the West Branch domain). Once through the Narrows, it is a drop into Penns Valley for the last few miles to Millheim. At the bottom of the mountain is the hamlet of Woodward, so tiny that you can hold your breath when entering and not breathe again until you have passed through. Woodward is the gateway to Woodward Cave, one of the state's biggest dry caverns.

Millheim and Aaronsburg, two Penns Valley towns almost next door to each other on U. S. Highway 45, are very small, typical in the respect of interior Pennsylvania's many Germanic settlements. Most villages are widely spaced through the valleys. Aaronsburg is the older of the two, laid out before 1775 by Aaron Levy of Sunbury. Aaronsburg, in its own deep little vale, once had ideas of becoming the state capital city. Wide setbacks and spacious lawns line the main street as it dips through town. Millheim, just over the next hill, is also cupped in a little hollow.

Farther west is the town known as State College, home to Penn State University, chartered in 1855. James Irvin, described by Penn State University as an "agriculturist and ironmaster . . . of Bellefonte," donated a two-hundred acre site for the campus and citizens of Centre and Huntingdon counties pledged $10,000 for the school. Eleven men comprised the first graduating class, receiving degrees identified as Bachelor of Scientific Agriculture. In 1871 six women were admitted as students, the first graduating in 1873. The growth of the University has been robust and has spread to what the University describes as "Penn State's new World Campus, which 'graduated' its first student in 2000, uses the Internet and other new technologies to offer instruction on an 'anywhere, anytime' basis." (*http://www.psu.edu/*).

The students of the University adopted the Nittany Lion as an athletic symbol in 1942, a reference to the mountain lion that once roamed the high hills. Nittany is a Native American word that refers to a *barrier* that protects. Mythology blends the Nittany Valley, the Nittany Mountain Range, and a romance between a white trader and an Indian maiden into a story that is worth holding onto. However, there is another story worth holding onto. During a baseball game between Princeton and Penn State in 1904, challenges of success volleyed between the teams. Penn State's Harrison D. "Joe" Mason (class of 1907) let it be known that the fearsome Nittany Mountain Lion would persevere, a title he alone created. Well, that title lasted and to this day the Nittany Lion will persevere and overshadow its enemy. Perhaps the "most famous class gift" donated to the students of the University arrived in 1940, the Nittany Lion Shrine, located on the University Park campus.

The nearby town of Bellefonte (a French word for *beautiful fountain*), just northeast of State College, snuggles up against long Bald Eagle Mountain. Supposedly the French statesman Charles Maurice de Talleyrand (1754 -1838) is responsible for the name, having made such a pronouncement when he saw the town's Big Spring, while on a visit during his exile from France in 1794 and 1795. The Big Spring is still a *belle fonte*, pouring forth millions of gallons of pure cold-mountain water daily. Limestone deposits in the area make up Bellefonte's economic industrial base. The town is a center for hunters, fishermen and farmers, too. Streets leading from the main thoroughfare literally climb up the side of the mountain, where houses hang on sometimes to improbable appearing perches.

Centre County and the counties around it are filled with a wide assortment of mountain and creek wilderness areas, some of them within the confines of state parks and recreation areas. Pennsylvanians like to remember the famous people, like Talleyrand, who visited or lived in the state for a time. One of the softly beautiful places in this mountain country is named for an illustrious man of letters. Poe Valley, just over the mountain south of Penns Valley and east of State College, honors Edgar Allen Poe, the builder of Gothic poems and stories. Poe lived in Philadelphia for a while, and during that time he visited with a relative who had settled in the valley area. Poe Valley is located out in the woods all by itself, watered by Penn's Creek and Little Poe Creek. It is here that the poet is believed to have written his famous poem *The Raven*. The valley is a lovely, lonely glade where two state recreation areas, Poe Valley State Park and Poe Paddy Park, offer a broad range of nature experiences. From a high ridge here, Penns View, famous over the state for its stunning purple-mountain vistas, look east to Bald Eagle Mountain and beyond. Mixed pine and hardwood forests swarm over the interwoven ridges far into the distance. The patented beauty of the scene varies with the seasonal color changes, but in one way it is always the same: awesome.

Penns View doesn't quite reach up to north-central Pennsylvania, and more is the pity. Here is the state's high plateau country, where autumn colors, when autumn arrives, are arranged in a different perspective. Due north from Poe country, some sixty miles in a straight line is Pennsylvania's "Grand Canyon," cut by a one-hundred mile-long Pine Creek that eventually reaches down to the West Branch of the Susquehanna River. Lycoming County Road 414 parallels the gorge to Blackwell in Tioga County, branching west to West Rim Road. At Leonard Harrison and Colton Point State Parks, flanking the gorge a few miles southwest of Wellsboro, the visitor may perch on the edge and direct his gaze downward a thousand feet, watching Pine Creek still at work. The steep, forested walls of the chasm are resplendent on a crisp autumn day, in gold and scarlet. The red-tailed hawk is king here; he soars over the magnificent gorge, his echoing eerie cry mingling with the splash of the rushing creek. This once was one of the East's most heavily logged mountain chasms; white pine was stripped from the slopes and floated down Pine Creek. The area's autumn colors are in part a legacy of the New Englanders who settled in north-central Pennsylvania for a while in the late 18th century, determined to annex the region to Connecticut. They brought their elms and sugar maple trees and planted them in-and-around the towns. Wellsboro, the gateway to the canyon, has many of these aged trees. The Yankees also built houses in the New England architectural style, and Wellsboro's architecture still reflects this influence with its Greek Revival columned porticos. The skirmishes between the New Englanders and the Pennsylvanians over this part of the state gave way after a while to the more critical business of starting a new nation. But this early incursion by the Connecticut Yankees has left a rich vein of New England that makes this spectacular forest and canyon country even more interesting than nature did all by herself.

State Parks

Pocono Mountains Region

Archbald Pothole State Park
    c/o Lackawanna State Park
    R. R. 1, Box 230
    Dalton, PA 18414

Beltzville State Park
    2950 Pohopoco Drive
    Lehighton, PA 18235

Big Pocono State Park
    c/o Tobyhanna State Park
    P. O. Box 387
    Tobyhanna, PA 18466

Frances Slocum State Park
    565 Mt. Olivet Road
    Wyoming, PA 18644

Gouldsboro State Park
    c/o Tobyhanna State Park
    P. O. Box 387
    Tobyhanna, PA 18466

Hickory Run State Park
    R. R. 1, Box 81
    White Haven, PA 18661

Lackawanna State Park
    R. R. 1, Box 230
    Dalton, PA 18414

Lehigh Gorge State Park
    c/o Hickory Run State Park
    R. R. 1, Box 81
    White Haven, PA 18661

Locust Lake State Park
    c/o Tuscarora State Park
    R. R. 1, Box 1051
    Barnesville, PA 18214

Mt. Pisgah State Park
    R. R. 3, Box 362A
    Troy, PA 16947

Nesopeck State Park
    c/o Hickory Run State Park
    R. R. 1, Box 81
    White Haven, PA 18661

Promised Land State Park
    R. R. 1, Box 96
    Greentown, PA 18426

Prompton State Park
    c/o Lackawanna State Park
    R. R.1, Box 230
    Dalton, PA 18414

Ricketts Glen State Park
    R. R. 2, Box 130
    Benton, PA 17814

Salt Spring State Park
    c/o Lackawanna State Park
    R. R. 1, Box 230
    Dalton, PA 18414

Tobyhanna State Park
    P. O. Box 387
    Tobyhanna, PA 18466

Tuscarora State Park
    R. R. 1, Box 1051
    Barnesville, PA 18214

Worlds End State Park
    P. O. Box 62
    Forksville, PA 18616

Philadelphia
and Surrounding Area

Benjamin Rush State Park
    2808 Three Mile Run Road
    Perkasie, PA 18944

Delaware Canal State Park
    11 Lodi Hill Road
    Upper Black Eddy, PA 18972

Evansburg State Park
    851 May Hall Road
    Collegeville, PA 19426

Fort Washington State Park
    500 Bethlehem Pike
    Fort Washington, PA 19034

Jacobsburg State Park
    835 Jacobsburg Road
    Wind Gap, PA 18091

Marsh Creek State Park
    675 Park Road
    Downingtown, PA 19335

Neshaminy State Park
    3401 State Road
    Bensalem, PA 19020

Nockamixon State Park
    1542 Mountain View Drive
    Quakertown, PA 18951

Norristown Farm Park State Park
    2808 Three Mile Run Road
    Perkasie, PA 18944

Ralph Stover State Park
    6011 State Park Road
    Pipersville, PA 18947

Ridley Creek State Park
Sycamore Mills Road
Media, PA 19063

Tyler State Park
101 Swamp Road
Newtown, PA 18940

White Clay Creek State Park
P. O. Box 172
Landenberg, PA 19350

Allegheny National Forest Region

Bendigo State Park
P. O. Box A
Glen Hazel Road
Johnsonburg, PA 15845

Bucktail State Park
R. R. 4, Box 212
Emporium, PA 15834

Chapman State Park
R. R. 2, Box 1610
Clarendon, PA 16313

Cherry Springs State Park
c/o Lyman Run State Park
454 Lyman Run Road
Galeton, PA 16922

Clear Creek State Park
R. R.1, Box 82
Sigel, PA 15860

Colton Point State Park
c/o Leonard Harrison S.P.
R. R. 6, Box 199
Wellsboro, PA 16901

Cook Forest State Park
P. O. Box 120, River Road
Cooksburg, PA 16217

Denton Hill State Park
Ski Denton
P. O. Box 367
Coudersport, PA 16915

Elk State Park
c/o Bendigo State Park
P. O. Box A, Glen Hazel Road
Johnsonburg, PA 15845

Hills Creek State Park
R. R. 2, Box 328
Wellsboro, PA 16901

Kinzua Bridge State Park
c/o Bendigo State Park
P. O. Box A, Glen Hazel Road
Johnsonburg, PA 15845

Leonard Harrison State Park
R. R. 6, Box 199
Wellsboro, PA 16901

Lyman Run State Park
454 Lyman Run Road
Galeton, PA 16922

Ole Bull State Park
HCR 62, Box 9
Cross Forks, PA 17729

Parker Dam State Park
R. R. 1, Box 165
Penfield, PA 15849

Patterson State Park
c/o Lyman Run State Park
454 Lyman Run Road
Galeton, PA 16922

Prouty Place State Park
c/o Lyman Run State Park
454 Lyman Run Road
Galeton, PA 16922

S. B. Elliott State Park
c/o Parker Dam State Park
R. R. 1, Box 165
Penfield, PA 15849

Sinnemahoning State Park
R. R. 1, Box 172
Austin, PA 16720

Sizerville State Park
R. R. 1, Box 238A
Emporium, PA 15834

Hershey—Dutch Country Region

Buchanan's Birthplace State Park
c/o Cowans Gap State Park
6235 Aughwick Road
Fort Loudon, PA 17224

Caledonia State Park
40 Rocky Mountain Road
Fayetteville, PA 17222

Codorus State Park
1066 Blooming Grove Road
Hanover, PA 17331

Colonel Denning State Park
1599 Doubling Gap Road
Newville, PA 17241

French Creek State Park
843 Park Road
Elverson, PA 19520

Gifford Pinchot State Park
2200 Rosstown Road
Lewisberry, PA 17339

Kings Gap State Park
500 Kings Gap Road
Carlisle, PA 17013

Memorial Lake State Park
R. R. 1, Box 7045
Grantville, PA 17028

Mont Alto State Park
c/o Caledonia State Park
40 Rocky Mountain Road
Fayetteville, PA 17222

Nolde Forest State Park
2910 New Holland Road
Reading, PA 19607

Pine Grove Furnace State Park
1100 Pine Grove Road
Gardners, PA 17324

Samuel S. Lewis State Park
c/o Gifford Pinchot State Park
2200 Rosstown Road
Lewisberry, PA 17339

Susquehannock State Park
c/o Gifford Pinchot State Park
2200 Rosstown Road
Lewisberry, PA 17339

Swatara State Park
c/o Memorial Lake State Park
R. R. 1, Box 7045
Grantville, PA 17028

Laurel Highlands
Southern Alleghenies

Blue Knob State Park
124 Park Road
Imler, PA 16655

Canoe Creek State Park
R. R. 2, Box 560
Hollidaysburg, PA 16648

Cowans Gap State Park
6235 Aughwick Road
Fort Loudon, PA 17224

Greenwood Furnace State Park
R. R. 2, Box 118
Huntingdon, PA 16652

Keystone State Park
R. R. 2, Box 101
Derry, PA 15627

Kooser State Park
943 Glades Pike
Somerset, PA 15501

Laurel Hill State Park
1454 Laurel Hill Park Road
Somerset, PA 15501

Laurel Mountain State Park
c/o Linn Run State Park
P. O. Box 50
Rector, PA 15677

Laurel Ridge State Park
1117 Jim Mountain Road
Rockwood, PA 15557

Laurel Summit State Park
c/o Linn Run State Park
P. O. Box 50
Rector, PA 15677

Linn Run State Park
P. O. Box 50
Rector, PAa 15677

Ohiopyle State Park
P. O. Box 105
Ohiopyle, PA 15470

Prince Gallitzin State Park
966 Marina Road
Patton, PA 16668

Ryerson Station State Park
R. R. 1, Box 77
Wind Ridge, PA 15380

Shawnee State Park
132 State Park Road
Schellsburg, PA 15559

Trough Creek State Park
R. R. 1, Box 211
James Creek, PA 16657

Warriors Path State Park
c/o Trough Creek State Park
R. R. 1, Box 211
James Creek, PA 16657

Whipple Dam State Park
c/o Greenwood Furnace S. P.
R. R. 2, Box 118
Huntingdon, PA 16652

Yellow Creek State Park
170 Route 259 Highway
Penn Run, PA 15765

Lake Erie Region

Maurice K. Goddard State Park
684 Lake Wilhelm Road
Sandy Lake, PA 16145

Oil Creek State Park
R. R. 1, Box 207
Oil City, PA 16301

Presque Isle State Park
P. O. Box 8510
Erie, PA 16505

Pymatuning State Park
2660 Williamsfield Road
Jamestown, PA 16134

Pittsburgh Region

Allegheny Island State Park
195 Park Road
Prospect, PA 16052

Hillman State Park
c/o Raccoon Creek State Park
3000 State Route 18
Hookstown, PA 15050

Jennings State Park
2951 Prospect Road
Slippery Rock, PA 16057

McConnell's Mill State Park
R. R. 2, Box 16
Portersville, PA 16051

Moraine State Park
225 Pleasant Valley Road
Portersville, PA 16051

Point State Park
101 Commonwealth Place
Pittsburgh, PA 15222

Raccoon Creek State Park
3000 State Route 18
Hookstown, PA 15050

Valleys of the Susquehanna

Bald Eagle State Park
149 Main Park Road
Howard, PA 16841

Big Spring State Park
c/o Colonel Denning State Park
1599 Doubling Gap Road
Newville, PA 17241

Black Moshannon State Park
R. R. 1, Box 183
Philipsburg, PA 16866

Colonel Denning State Park
1599 Doubling Gap Road
Newville, PA 17241

Fowlers Hollow State Park
c/o Colonel Denning State Park
1599 Doubling Gap Road
Newville, PA 17241

Hyner Run State Park
P. O. Box 46
Hyner, PA 17738

Hyner View State Park
c/o Hyner Run State Park
P. O. Box 46
Hyner, PA 17738

Kettle Creek State Park
HCR 62, Box 96
Renovo, PA 17764

Little Buffalo State Park
R. R. 2, Box 256A
Newport, PA 17074

Little Pine State Park
4205 Little Pine Creek Road
Waterville, PA 17776

McCall Dam State Park
c/o R. B. Winter State Park
R. R. 2, Box 314
Mifflinburg, PA 17844

Milton State Park
c/o Shikellamy State Park
Bridge Avenue
Sunbury, PA 17801

Penn Roosevelt State Park
c/o Greenwood Furnace S.P.
R. R. 2, Box 118
Huntingdon, PA 16652

Poe Paddy State Park
c/o Poe Valley State Park
1405 New Lancaster Valley Rd
Milroy, PA 17063

Poe Valley State Park
c/o Reeds Gap State Park
1405 New Lancaster Valley Rd
Milroy, PA 17063

R. B. Winter State Park
R. R. 2, Box 314
Mifflinburg, PA 17844

Ravensburg State Park
c/o R. B. Winter State Park
R. R. 2, Box 314
Mifflinburg, PA 17844

Reeds Gap State Park
1405 New Lancaster Valley Rd
Milroy, PA 17063

Sand Bridge State Park
c/o R. B. Winter State Park
R. R. 2, Box 314
Mifflinburg, PA 17844

Shikellamy State Park
Bridge Avenue
Sunbury, PA 17801

Susquehanna State Park
1500 W.Third Street
Williamsport, PA 17701

Upper Pine Bottom State Park
c/o Little Pine State Park
4205 Little Pine Creek Road
Waterville, PA 17776